Unseen Work:

Why the best path to your goals is not always a straight line

Myles J. Biggs

FOR MY FAMILY

While your support may be Unseen to many, it will never be lost on me. Your love means more to me than you will ever know – or words can express.

CONTENTS

PREFACE:
A NOTE FROM THE AUTHOR

I killed myself.

Metaphorically.

Eight months before my thirtieth birthday.

I woke up one day and had an epiphany. It was as if I had been jolted awake from a bizarre dream or an out of body experience. I could see a version of myself making terrible decisions and ridiculous rationalizations. When I finally woke up and looked around, I barely recognized my own life.

From the outside looking in, I had it all. A high-powered career, six-figure salary, loving wife, beautiful baby boy, a brand-new home on acres of land, the respect of my peers, and seemingly nowhere else to go but up. At face value — all true. But deep down, I knew the truth. My gut was screaming at me each morning -- literally.

I woke up every morning to intense panic attacks that brought me to my knees and face-to-face with the almighty porcelain throne. Each new day would begin with me heaving into the toilet whatever had managed to escape my digestive system overnight. Now, doesn't that sound like a guy who has it all?

After seeking help to discern why I was feeling this way, and after many months more of work on myself, it became clear that I had been chasing, and living, a life that I only *thought* I wanted. I had spent years slaving away to live up to others' expectations and had not paid attention to the lamenting of my inner creator. Eventually, and somewhat sadistically, he made sure I heard his screams.

Rock bottom for me was when I had to take my first antidepressant to simply get through a normal day of my own life. I placed the blue oval on the tip of my tongue, kicked it back, and exhaled deeply. As my head came forward, my glance rested in the mirror upon the piercing eyes of a stranger. Before me, all I could see was the hollow shell of a person living his life for other people and not for himself – every under-eye wrinkle chronicling years spent denying the truth and foregoing the pursuit of fulfillment in favor of *success.*

At that exact moment — I erased that stranger.

Since that day, I've begun the rigorous and rewarding process of deciding who the new me will be. I've been determined to bring this intense level of awareness into every aspect of my life and to never again feel like a stranger in my own skin. I've also resolved to share my own journey as openly as possible, through my podcast and now these pages, so that others know they are not alone in their inner struggles.

Life does not have to be as hard as we make it!

I've shared this bathroom mirror scene with you, not to make you feel sorry for me, but so that you know things like this can be overcome. In the timespan of one year, I used that rock-bottom moment to completely re-architect my life and lean into my passions with all I have.

Here's the not-so-secret truth – you can too!

The pages that follow are a compilation of what others have taught me (without even realizing it), and what I have learned, both for and about myself, along the way. Perhaps the most freeing insight gained from uncovering my own Unseen Work is the realization that there is actually no destination. The idea that we will all one day "make it" and be completely satisfied with our accomplishments, at some metaphorical finish line, is a complete illusion.

We live in a world where everyone is hurling themselves towards this arbitrary finish line which only teases its close proximity. Just when we think the end is within reach, it gleefully skips off into the distance once more.

This awareness has made me focus on relishing the journey towards that dynamic checkered flag. At the end of the day, our *pursuit* of success is truly all we have. Our own definitions of perfection will continue to evolve and will always place themselves just out of reach. Learning to be okay with this notion is the source of true fulfillment and joy.

If you're unsure of what you want; if you feel stuck, frustrated, stressed, or anxious; if you feel alone inside, even though to outsiders, you appear to have it all – take a deep breath. I have been where you are. Please know that you do not have to accept this way of existing as the prison sentence it often mimics.

As you read this book, my hope for you is that you are able to take inventory of your life and your circle of influences. Most importantly, I hope to show you the power of your own thoughts. If you walk away from this book with even the smallest morsel of an insight into your own motivations, I've accomplished what I have set out to do.

I can promise you this: by identifying and leaning into the Unseen Work in your life, you are, in fact, preparing yourself to be *seen*. Once you let go of that societally-imposed destination in the distance and learn to find joy in the miracle of each, weary step of the journey, the warmth of your well-earned spotlight will feel as inviting as the summer sun on your face. You will be able to step outside of your comfort zone and stretch your belief in what you are capable of. Just imagine:

What if you had no discomfort zone?

Ultimately, when we can become comfortable with the

uncomfortable, the shackles of societal expectations fall away, and we are able to exceed the wildest of our own expectations. If you can give yourself over to this process, then, my friends, both you and the world will never again be the same.

I'm honored to be invited along for your journey, and I am grateful that you are giving me the opportunity to share a piece of mine.

Most sincerely yours,

Myles

P.S. I urge you not to treat this book as a static object. Scribble in the margins, highlight your favorite stories and use what you find inside as the launch pad for the next chapter of your journey. I want to hear from you as you do! In the back pages you will find all my contact information – my REAL contact information. I'd be honored at the opportunity to answer your questions or help you work through elements of your own Unseen Work.

INTRODUCTION:
MY 'WHY'

Ironically, the process of writing this book consisted of what is perhaps the greatest amount of Unseen Work I have ever done: nearly three years of podcasting, over a year of writing and editing, and countless hours spent reading other authors in search of inspiration.

Another irony – this book wasn't even my own idea! It was suggested, in passing, by an acquaintance of mine in an online mastermind program. In the early days of my writing process, I never actually thought I would finish it. However, once the words began to flow from my mind to the page, the theme of Unseen Work seemed to take root in my subconscious.

It followed me to the gym each morning, throughout the workday each week and would even wake me up at night. Unable to shake the idea, I had no choice but to finish writing it down. I found myself inspired to write in the oddest places – driving my car (using talk-to-text features, of course), walking my dog and even in the middle of conversations with other people. My phone is filled with small notes and fleeting thoughts that were eventually compiled into the pages that follow.

The entire process and journey of becoming an author has humbled me. I've battled the voice in my head, questioning just who I think I am and why I think I am special enough to write a book. I've asked myself questions, like:

Why do I even want to write a book?

Who am I writing this book for?

What do I expect to come of the process?

What will make this book stand out as special?

In the beginning of the process, these questions seemed to recklessly bounce off the darkest corners of my mind, occasionally squeezing through the doorway between my unconscious and conscious thoughts. Each one forcing my attention and demanding answers. In an effort to build our newly formed author-reader relationship, I feel it's only fair to give you some insight into my answers to these questions; if nothing else, as a way to share a bit of my own Unseen Work.

In the beginning, I was convinced that I was writing this book only for myself. To prove to myself that I could do it. However, as the process continued on, I realized that this book wasn't just for *me*, but for anyone who's had a moment like I did staring back at a stranger in the bathroom mirror. Having soldiered on and erased my personal stranger, I feel it is my duty to now help others to do the same.

This book is also for my children. I want them to grow up knowing that you really can do anything you not only put your mind to, but also take actions toward. Someday, when I am gone from this world, my children, and perhaps even by grandchildren, will be able to keep this piece of me with them.

I don't expect anything from publishing this book. And in a way, I find that beautiful. The reward for me is not in the destination. I've already earned my reward. And that is in creating the pages you hold (you'll understand this perspective better at the end, I promise).

While many books have been written on similar topics, this is the only book that has ever been written by me (so far!). It's written about my life. It's written about what I have learned from hundreds of conversations with amazing people and hours of my own Unseen Work. While there may be other books, written by others on similar subjects — this one is uniquely my own.

I'm on a mission to change the world by changing myself. And, by doing so, inspire others to do the same and reassure them that they are not alone. This is why I wrote this book.

Put simply, I believe that each and every one of us is capable of greatness and of harnessing our creative passions. For me, the mere fact that we, as human beings, have been *created* is part of what drives this urge to further all of creation. Whatever adding to creation looks like for you, it is my sincere hope that by channeling your Unseen Work you can not only achieve it, but have fun getting there. Furthermore, after drawing upon an awareness of your own Unseen Work, I hope that you notice the unseen struggles of every person you encounter and extend them as much grace as possible. If we can all switch our focus from short term satisfaction to an appreciation for the long game of Unseen Work, the possibilities are infinite.

LAYING THE FOUNDATION

As a husband, father, son, brother, employee, entrepreneur, podcaster, speaker, coach, and now writer, I know how precious the hours in each day are, and I am grateful you are choosing to spend them with me.

As I have alluded to already, this book is the natural evolution of a podcasting journey I began in 2017. Much like my decision to write this book, one day I simply decided that podcasting was something I wanted to try. So, I did. All these years later, I never would have guessed that small decision would lead to this moment and to countless others I now cherish. Truly, those *unseen* connections are what this book is about.

As we explore this idea that I call Unseen Work, I will continue to pepper in my own personal anecdotes amongst those from the people I have met on my journey.

The phrase Unseen Work, itself, came to me in an off-the-cuff, rambling mess of a response to an open-ended question posed to me about mindset. I was trying to verbalize a theme I had noticed emerging in almost all my podcast episodes. On my podcast, *Relish The Journey*, I've interviewed CEOs and motivational speakers, contestants from TV shows like *Chopped* and *Shark Tank*, music producers with songs airing on award winning shows, up and coming singer songwriters from Nashville, Rabbis, authors, the list goes on and on.

Some folks still held down full-time jobs while building incredible passion projects – these people all did, or are actively doing, things that no one would begin to guess. They all started from somewhere humble. And they all had their fair share of Unseen Work before their first big break. Or any, big break for that matter. Over time, it has become apparent to me that, while successful people may project an incredible facade of confidence, as I have dug deeper into interview questions, I have found that the same distinct insecurities would begin to emerge among all of my guests. Further, they all had stories of their days in the trenches that felt all too similar to the current state of my own life.

Early in this book writing process, as if by divine intervention, I stumbled upon an application for a TEDx event in Williamsport, Pennsylvania -- home of the Little League Baseball World Series, the city where I went to school (shout out Lycoming College). Every TED event (which stands for Technology, Entertainment and Design) features speakers from a multitude of disciplines, all speaking on one overarching topic. The Williamsport event was accepting speaker applications on topics which fit under the umbrella of "The Next Chapter." As I was perusing the online speaking forms, it dawned on me that in order to get to the next chapter, it took Unseen Work. This phrase that had just fallen out of my mouth only a few days prior now had intense meaning. I dove into the application process without pausing to think twice and hit "send" on the application thirty minutes later.

Then I forgot about it. It sounds cliché. But I truly did.

I went about my day-to-day routine and figured that, if nothing else, the process of applying had given me a great head start on fleshing out the book idea. But, as fate would have it, I got an email a few weeks later saying that I had passed the written portion of the application process and was now invited to proceed to the second round. This new obstacle consisted of a five-minute speech which would have to be delivered in person. Auditions were one month away, and I would be required to deliver my talk in front of a panel of TEDx organizers and judges. Immediately following my talk, I would have to answer a battery of interview questions surrounding my motivations for seeking a speaker's slot.

I immediately put book writing on hold and pivoted to speech writing. My process was a bit unconventional, but it worked. Instead of actually writing, I sat down in my podcast studio and rambled incessantly until I had nothing left to say. Then, I played the recording back and typed feverishly. After my initial edit, I read back what I had written and recorded it once more. I was now the proud owner of a ten-minute TEDx talk. From there, every morning and evening when I walked my dog, I listened back to the speech. I also listened to it in the gym, on repeat, for an hour each morning. I did this for about a week. All the while, writing additional ideas in the notepad on my phone or dictating additional audio messages to myself. After a week of this, I sat down for a two-hour editing marathon, slashing and rewriting and slashing some more. The result was the following script, which clocked in at exactly four minutes and forty-four seconds.

One month after receiving that email of congratulations, issuing the new challenge, I stood on stage and confidently delivered the following script alongside the dueling internal emotions of fear, anxiety and excitement:

Throughout two years of podcasting I have recorded over 100 episodes and interviewed almost as many people. Across all of these conversations, it did not matter who I was interviewing, or where they were from, or how successful they were, one theme always emerged as a constant. And that is what I am excited to explore with you all today.

But first, let me ask you something – have you ever picked up a book and skipped to the last chapter? Or put on a new movie and fast forwarded to the final scene? Your answer to either of these is most likely a resounding "no."

Because without experiencing the beginning or the middle, there is no way we can appreciate the end of any story. Including, and especially, our own.

Interesting then that society pays little attention to the beginning or middle and is obsessed with the ending. We call it – success. This focus on who has "made it" has us judging each other based on follower counts or post views and actively coveting the newest status symbol: all in search of validation.

But, instead of trying to recreate what our idols have achieved, we should instead chase what they did to reach the top. Instead of focusing on "making it," we should glorify the process of Unseen Work.

While building my podcast, I've shadowed successful entrepreneurs who spent years eating nothing but PB&J and pinching pennies before seeing any success in business.

Unseen Work.

I've spoken with singer songwriters in Nashville who have written hundreds of songs before anyone took notice of their talents.

Unseen Work.

And I've interviewed reality-TV contestants who spent years honing a craft before stepping out on camera for a literal fifteen minutes of fame.

Unseen Work.

They all persisted when no one was watching, so that, when they were seen, they had something to show for it.

An excellent example of Unseen Work comes to us from mother nature.

If you were to plant a bamboo seed, it could take up to five years of watering and soil cultivation before you saw any sprouting begin.

During this time your neighbors, friends and family may laugh and question why you're wasting your time on something that's obviously not working.

But, when five years and one day comes along, that plant, which has been growing an extensive root system beneath the surface for five, seemingly uneventful years, can grow to be up to 80 feet tall in just six weeks. It's the Unseen Work that happens beneath the soil that propels this exponential growth.

Now your neighbors, your friends and your family will all want their own bamboo. Instead of laughing at you, they are asking how you did it.

If we were to only focus that Instagrammable photo of our 80-foot-tall bamboo tree, instead of enjoying the disciplined routine required to make it a reality, we could spend five years wrestling with self-doubt, anxiety or even depression. We might even give in to all of the external pressure to quit this thing that's obviously not working. Or making any money.

Sound familiar?

Most of the time we focus on these external pressures and sources of negativity, when in reality our internal dialogue can be the most damning. These thoughts, these voices inside our heads, are perhaps the most common type of Unseen Work. The things we tell ourselves and no one else. These thoughts become our beliefs, our beliefs affect our actions and our actions determine our level of success.

I'd like us to focus on that internal voice right now. Humor me please and close your eyes. Just focus on my voice and tune out all other distractions.

Now, I'd like you to visualize a goal you have for yourself. What's that bamboo plant you've been trying to grow? Bring that into focus and zero in on it in your mind's eye.

When you can see it clearly, ask yourself:

Who will you have to become to make this a reality?

How will you feel when you finally achieve it?

What daily habits will you have to take consistent and disciplined action upon to get there?

What Unseen Work will it take?

When you're ready, open your eyes please.

I want you to realize that if you feel alone in your pursuits – you're not. You're just unseen. And that's ok. Use this invisibility to your advantage and fail as much as you can and as fast as you can. But keep persisting, keep learning, keep growing that extensive root system beneath the surface.

But no matter what, I challenge you to never lose sight of that future you just created for yourself when your eyes were closed. You have to do the Unseen Work, so that when you are seen, you have something to show for it.

I began this unseen process of writing, editing and practicing the speech in my bathroom mirror and kept it all to myself for nearly a month. When I decided to let the words see the light of day and gave practice speeches in front of family and friends, the response was so profound that I decided it was, in fact, worth exploring further. Because of that initial feedback, the five-minute speech you just read now serves at the foundation for the pages which follow.

As for the audition – I crushed it. I earned a spot at the TEDx 2020 event in Williamsport, Pennsylvania. To view my full presentation, search "Unseen Work Myles Biggs TEDx" on YouTube or visit my website: www.mylesbiggs.com.

TYPES OF UNSEEN WORK

Armed with the new framework outlined from my TEDx talk, I found myself noticing Unseen Work in all of my personal interactions and not just in my podcast episodes. Not dissimilar to when you buy a new car and then feel like you see it all around you when you never noticed it before your purchase. I found myself striking up regular, in person conversations with friends and family about the idea outside of my podcast interviews and even started using an "Unseen Work" line of questioning with new podcast guests.

As a result of this ad-hoc, qualitative and completely unscientific research, I've identified three main categories of Unseen Work. To be sure, there are plenty of sub-categories, but these three serve as excellent umbrellas for the conversation to live under:

1. Generational Unseen Work
2. Active Unseen Work
3. Passive Unseen Work

Generational Unseen Work: The only reason any of us even have the opportunity to pursue our own Unseen Work journeys is because of those who came before us. This type of Unseen Work is often invisible even to ourselves. It's the hard-fought lessons of our parents and grandparents, their parents and grandparents, and beyond. An awareness of Generational Unseen Work will make it clear that what we may call "luck" is really the result of our ancestor's resilience. Ultimately, each generation stands on the shoulders of the generation that came before them. This type of Unseen Work begins before our earliest memories. Even the seemingly invisible or mundane happenings from our youth cumulate over the years and result in the foundation for the way we view the world and how we show up in it.

Active Unseen Work: Building on the foundation of Generational Unseen Work, this is a knowing focus on and pursuit of a specific goal. It takes place when we are aware of the fact that we are on a journey towards a well-defined end and we are taking purposeful steps to achieve what we've set out to accomplish. Continuing our education with a degree, developing and executing a specific plan within our careers or even cleaning our homes all contain elements of Active Unseen Work. Most people only see the diploma, successful corporate event or dog-hair free living room – what they do not see is what it took to reach those milestones. Active Unseen Work reinforces the idea that, while you learn *about* something by studying it, you learn how to *do* something by actively doing it. When we begin our Unseen Work with a destination in mind, we take one invisible, yet active, step after another until we can stand in the spotlight.

Passive Unseen Work: If Active Unseen Work begins with the end in mind, Passive Unseen Work is simply choosing to begin, without knowing where your efforts may take you. This consists of seemingly unrelated lessons and experiences that, when added together, produce a significant preparedness for a moment in time we never knew would arrive. By its name, Passive Unseen Work may seem like the contrarian to Active Unseen Work, however it is ultimately the accumulation of unrelated active pursuits, the cross fertilization and compounding of each experience in unique ways. These are the "hindsight is 20/20" moments of our lives. The connecting of our own dots. As we look back on trials, tribulations, and triumphs, we can now see how they brought us to a current success. But, in the moment, we curse them with a creative string of expletives which (hopefully) also remains unseen.

I've learned to love Passive Unseen Work the most. After you finish this book and become aware of the Unseen Work in your own lives, I hope it becomes yours as well. Passive Unseen Work is the journey. If you're lucky enough to fall in love with the unending process of pursuing a higher goal, it doesn't matter if you ever reach the initial finish line you've selected for yourself, because, as you'll discover for yourself, the reward is in who you become while charging towards that line. Not in crossing it. Most often, we even achieve things far greater than the initial goal.

Take me for example.

Years ago, I decided to start my podcast. Purely on a whim. I had no idea what I was doing and fumbled through dozens of episodes with family and friends before building up the confidence to reach outside of my inner circle for guests. Smash cut to today, and years of interviewing complete strangers has completely transformed my confidence level and my own personal brand; to the point where I have led interactive presentations on international stages and have given a TEDx Talk. And now you're reading my book! As I look back on my own journey, it's easy to see how each invisible step helped prepare me for the next opportunity. But, if I had waited for the path to perfectly reveal itself before I ever recorded one podcast episode, we would not be sharing this sentence together.

Bridging the G.A.P.: These three types of Unseen Work are not mutually exclusive. Active and Passive work do not exist in a vacuum and our Generational Unseen Work is nothing more than the Active and Passive Unseen Work of our ancestors. Likewise, Passive Unseen Work is often the compounding of unrelated instances of Active Unseen Work. This book arranges the three types of Unseen Work into the above order on purpose. When presented in this way — Generational, Active and Passive — we can take the first letter of each to form an acronym: G.A.P. Later on in this book, after we have dissected the three types of Unseen Work in detail, we will look at examples and stories of how we can leverage all three to bridge an invisible G.A.P. found all around each of us, separating our perceived and actual realities.

Early in my podcasting career, someone shared this quote with me from the famed motivational speaker Jim Rohn:

"You're the average of the five people you spend the most time with."

I love this quote so much. This book serves to add my own twist to it. I believe that, not only are you the average of the five people you spend the most time with, but *you are the sum of all of your interactions with those people.*

Ultimately, the person you actually spend the most time with is yourself. Therefore, the investment of your precious time with the highest rate of return is the time spent working to better yourself. Time spent pursuing self-mastery. Time spent developing a much keener awareness of the motivators behind all of your actions. In many ways, this is the ultimate Unseen Work.

To best illustrate this idea, and to further explain the three areas of Unseen Work and then how the three of them can be leveraged in unison, this book will draw upon stories from my podcast guests and from my own life. In order to properly highlight areas of Unseen Work, certain details and examples taken from my podcast guests may be exaggerated. In some instances, I might over exaggerate these details to make a point or to expedite our arrival at key points. All of this was done with consent from each guest, and in some cases, through collaboration with them to ensure that any exaggeration or inference still embodied the truth of their stories.

Furthermore, storytelling will be the medium in which I share many of these lessons learned. Each section will begin with a bit of a short story focusing on a specific aspect of someone's Unseen Work. Then we will dissect the lessons to be learned. Finally, we will unpack how we can compound the lessons from each story into the overarching lessons of the Unseen Work types.

At the end of each section, I have created journaling prompts to assist you in mapping out your own Unseen Work. My hope is that these stories, paired with the lessons they have taught me and the lessons you'll unearth in your own journaling practice, will help you unlock the power of Unseen Work in your daily life.

PART 1:
GENERATIONAL UNSEEN WORK

CHAPTER 1:
THE MATRIARCH

On February 14, 1938, the world received a precious Valentine — Marion Kuber. Born into a family of Polish immigrants, Marion grew up knowing the intense love and connectedness of family. In fact, her entire family shared a home in Brooklyn, seven of them in total: three grandparents, her parents and her brother. Today this sounds like the makings of a Netflix original series, but back then it was a common situation. It also meant that, whether she liked it or not, family would be a keystone in every area of her childhood.

Marion's parents met and fell in love where they both worked, the Silver Cup Baking Company. Her grandfather worked in a pencil factory, also within walking distance of their home: bringing home rejects from the production line to share with his grandchildren. No doubt a carry-over precaution from the days of the Great Depression, when something as simple as a pencil became a luxury and was difficult to afford.

Also, within walking distance was the community church. On Sunday mornings, the air was filled with a cacophony of sounds: the tolling of church bells, the laughter of children, the chatter of adults and the collective echoing of feet on pavement as entire city blocks filed in to give thanks. Marion's family wasn't the only family living with multiple generations under one roof. This sense of family extended well beyond their own four walls, with the church at the center of their small Brooklyn community.

For entertainment, the entire family enjoyed a first-generation record player. Evenings were spent reading, sharing thoughtful conversation or perched on the floor in front of the radio's speaker, listening to the sounds of shows and allowing imagination to paint the picture. Later in her youth, from time to time, the entire family would spend an evening at a local neighbor's house who had sprung for a television.

Certainly, a different era than our world today!

During World War II, New York City was seen as a crucial piece of the United States economy — that much has not changed. However, while our focus today is on virtual warfare, with the threat of enemy troops violating our sovereignty rarely discussed as an actual possibility, back then the memory of Pearl Harbor was still fresh, and tensions were high. As a child, Marion was forced to draw dark drapes at night, with the thought being that enemy aircraft would not be able to identify urban areas for air assaults if they could not use lights to assist in targeting. Her family was issued ration books for the necessities at the grocery store and joined the entire country in feeling the pain of war. That same community still funneled into church pews on Sunday, but the collective chatter among the adults was much less cheerful than in the days before the war.

However, all of that focus on negative possibilities didn't stop Marion from the joys of adolescence. She enjoyed going bowling and dancing with her friends.

In fact, as early as 15 years of age, Marion and her friends would take the bus into Manhattan to attend dances with their friends. While the entire world may have been wrapped up in rebounding from the depression or launching into war, Marion was a normal teenager focused on having fun with friends, pursuing her passions and honoring her family. She also turned to her education as an escape from the seemingly unstable world stage. This escape proved fruitful as she found herself at the top of her class and the proud recipient of a scholarship to a prominent Catholic high school. It would take her two public busses and over half an hour to get to that school each day, but that didn't bother her in the slightest. She flourished there, excelling in her studies and even joining the young dramatics club — marrying her love of both music and dance with the intellectual prowess required to memorize scripts.

It was 1958, at one of these New York City dances at the Manhattan Club (where they had continuous polka music playing well into the night), that Marion met the man she would later marry. They were introduced by a mutual friend, danced together several times and an undeniable connection formed. Just one year later they were married and had their first daughter.

Being a mother was always Marion's dream. Growing up surrounded by family had always made her look forward to having one of her own and she threw herself into motherhood with true vigor. She moved from Brooklyn to New Jersey with her husband and the dancing duo were eventually blessed with four, healthy daughters. Marion opted to stay home to raise their children as her husband built up a family business.

When their daughters were school-aged, Marion went to work at the family business, putting her intellectual mind to work keeping the books and organizing the office. As Marion would say: she loved to straighten out messes.

While the focus would often be on her husband, who was the face of the company, Marion also went to school and earned the same business certifications that he possessed, which were required to run the company. They decided, as a team, that this was necessary. In case anything prevented him from working, she would be able to run the company. In decades where women had to fight tooth and nail to be taken seriously in business, Marion always had a seat at the table.

Later in life, she would put this business acumen to work once more; running a thrift shop which supported the local hospital system through its earnings. There, she would train and oversee a team of volunteers, organize and categorize a constant influx of retail merchandise and implement systems to cut costs in an effort to ensure as much money as possible was donated to fund life-saving programs. Her efforts were rewarded numerous times with regional and national awards for philanthropy and leadership.

Now in her 80s, she continues to feed her brain: devouring enormous books on historical figures like Abraham Lincoln, keeping up to date with the newest forms of technology as a way to video chat with her great grandchildren and by providing counsel as the matriarch of a family now over 25 in number. All these years later, Marion has never lost that grit she cultivated in Brooklyn; and, not surprisingly, it has found its way into the DNA of her entire family.

CHAPTER 2:
THE ENTREPRENEUR

As one of 10 children, Mickey Hergert was born in July of 1933 and grew up in Linden, New Jersey. To ensure the large family had all of the essentials, his father worked during the day as a police officer, and often at night as a bus driver. Mickey's father may not have always been around for a game of catch, but his focus was constantly on what could be done to support the family. His mother worked in the home and tended to the family's bustling brood of children; doing her best to shelter her kids from the harsh realities of life and the stressful adult responsibilities that come with raising ten children on the heels of an economic depression. Somehow, in the midst of raising her ten children and acting as the homemaker, she also opened a successful restaurant next to their house: catering to the local factory workers with homemade hot meals. One of Mickey's chores was to take his bike on the one-mile trek to the bakery to pick up fresh goods for the restaurant, then make the ride back in time for the breakfast rush.

The rest of the world may have been suffering from a societal and economic depression, but the Hergert clan was happy. Sure, they were all working and finding ways to contribute towards putting food on the table, but they had each other for support. And, frankly, there was no other option. This was life for most families back then. Free from the yoke of comparison, they simply chose to find enjoyment in the midst of the daily rat race.

As children of two hard working parents, Mickey and his nine siblings grew up to not just understand the fruits of entrepreneurship but see them in action each and every day. Although, back then, it didn't have that fancy title, it was just known as survival.

When Mickey was in the sixth grade, his father enlisted him to help with a carpentry project. Today, for most sixth graders, a carpentry project would consist of building a pinewood derby car. For Mickey, it meant going to work helping his father build a new, two-story home onto the existing family restaurant. Upon completion of the project, the entire family of twelve people took up residence in that home.

Up until that year, Mickey had attended a private Catholic school. But now, having created something with his own two hands, he was infatuated with woodworking. So much so that he asked his parents to transfer to a different school that had woodshop, metal shop and mechanical drawing. Since he knew carpentry was what he wanted to do with his life, he figured it didn't make sense to wait before getting started. So, he dove in.

And he excelled.

So much so, that in his junior year, Mickey left high school to join a carpentry union. Again, while most seventeen-year old children today are worrying about buying the correct brand name sneaker so they fit in at school, or how many views their Tik-Tok video receives, Mickey was building a career and putting food on the table to feed his family.

He arrived at his first job site on his bicycle (the same one which used to make those daily trips to the bakery) and without any tools. Since he didn't quite know what he was going to be doing, and there weren't piles of extra cash around to purchase unnecessary tools, he wanted to wait and see what he would absolutely *need* before making any investments.

At first glance, his supervisor thought he was a lost schoolboy loitering on the jobsite and not his newest apprentice. Since Mickey did not have any tools, the supervisor put him to work in the only available position — the mill. Here he used the same two hands that helped build his family's home to move, stack and cut lumber all day. After a few short weeks in the mill, Mickey now had intimate knowledge of every piece of wood that went into building a home, he had also mastered the difficult task of laying out rafters for the roof; a skill that required as much math and mental acuity as it did brute strength.

Having now proven his work ethic, and purchased proper tools, he was cycled through every position on the job site; beginning with hammering nails into the subfloor and then, literally, working his way up — all the way up to the roof. Mickey spent three years on that residential job site. He loved every minute of it! Each day he added new skills to his metaphorical (and sometimes actual) tool belt. His passion for, and knowledge of his craft, grew and grew.

One day, he and his crew were tasked with building a home that had a unique roofline and required each roof rafter to be laid out on-site and cut one at a time. Normally the rafters were cut off-site and then delivered to the job for assembly. Of the five-man crew, many of whom had significantly more experience than he, Mickey was the only one who knew how to get the job done — thanks to those early days in the mill. Ironically, his initial lack of physical tools helped him to cultivate the greatest tool a carpenter should have – an analytical mind.

On payday that week, Mickey was surprised to find extra cash in his envelope. Being the good former Catholic-school boy that he was, he approached his supervisor, presented the extra cash and claimed that a mistake must have been made. With a wry smile and a smack on the back, the supervisor shared with Mickey that he happened to be looking out the window at the precise moment he was laying out a complex rafter system – by himself – with the rest of the crew simply watching. The extra cash was a raise for a job well done and that was no mistake. Bolstered by this exchange, Mickey worked even harder.

Upon completion of this residential housing project he followed the same developer to a spot on the Hudson river with a direct sightline to New York City. Significantly different than a residential project, this jobsite featured an array of six, five-story buildings. Here, he expanded his skills beyond wood and learned how to work with metal and pour concrete. He also got the opportunity to work on building factories and other challenging pieces of architecture in addition to residential homes.

At just 23 years-old, Mickey already had six years of experience in his trade. He decided to put the skills he normally employed for someone else's job site into his own project and set out to build his own house. It would be a 22-foot x 33-foot bungalow with a carport and would be situated directly across the street from the Barnegat Bay in Waretown, New Jersey. The perfect place for a small summer cottage and a break from the hard labor of construction.

At the time, General Motors was building a few projects nearby. While the projects were in progress, the company would construct small shanties to serve as changing rooms for employees. As the jobs neared completion, these structures were dismantled, and the pieces put at the curb for trash. All these years later, Mickey's father had not lost the resourceful mindset bestowed upon him by the Great Depression and he counseled his son to go see what could be used out of this "trash." Like any good son would, he listened to his father, took the backseat out of his car, and loaded it up with "trash" week after week. It would take months, and dozens of trips, but eventually Mickey's stockpile of recycled building supplies, bolstered by a few additions from the local hardware store, would be enough to build his house.

As his career progressed, in addition to building homes, Mickey would go on to both sell them as a real estate broker and offer insurance packages for them. He built his own office building and founded his own company, the Hergert Agency, which would eventually employ over 15 real estate agents. Mickey would go on to serve as a city councilman for over a decade and was appointed to the New Jersey Real Estate Commission, where he served for almost the same length of time. While he grew up in an era of economic depression, he would eventually amass a personal fortune — more than enough to retire at an early age. However, he would instead choose to work at his real estate company until the age of 76 years young. To this day, in his mid-eighties, if there is a job to be done, you'll find Mickey on the move.

CHAPTER 3:
MARION & MICKEY

When Mickey was working on those commercial buildings across the Hudson from New York City, he and his compatriots would often venture across the river in search of nightly entertainment. Where did the rough and gruff construction workers go for a fun night on the town? Believe it or not — dancing. Mickey's ancestors hailed from both Poland and Germany and music was a big part of his childhood, specifically polka music. He and his friends often sought out music and dance halls known for hosting events featuring his up-tempo dance of choice.

On one such night, the Manhattan Club was hosting a night of continuous Polka music. When one dance ended, another began immediately. Those in attendance rotated dance partners with expert precision. That evening, one of Mickey's dance partners encouraged him to take a turn dancing with her friend. She thought the two of them would have a lot in common and would get along well — both on the dance floor, and off of it. After some prodding, he accepted the nudging to ask her to dance. *That woman was Marion Kuber.*

As Mickey recounts the story, Marion was wearing a dress with three medals embroidered on the front. He saw this as a conversation starter. After introducing himself, he politely, and perhaps a bit sarcastically, asked her what the medals meant. Immediately matching his wit, she responded by saying that they were for "good behavior."

This would be the point in the movie where a beam of light dramatically began to focus on the two of them as they shared smiles and sets of twinkling eyes. While the world around them was full of frenetic and fast-paced Polka dancing, in the space between them, time would stand still. The duo would go from sharing a dance together, to sharing a life together — they were married a year, almost to the day, after that first encounter.

The two never lost their love of the Polka. On Saturday mornings, Mickey would take joy in donning his metaphorical chef's hat and whipping up a big Polish breakfast of kielbasa (sausage), szynka (ham), eggs, pastries, and arguably the greasiest and best breakfast potatoes you've ever tasted. No doubt going back in time to that family-owned restaurant he so often assisted in. When the meal was nearing completion, he would crank up the Polka music and awaken his four daughters and bride with this indescribable mix of horns and hash browns.

In addition to building their family, Mickey and Marion also built a successful business together. Marion was at Mickey's side as he studied for his real estate license, built up the family business and pursued his political offices, which inevitably helped to network him deeper into the community and fuel his real estate ventures. As a team, the two of them built a real estate empire, raised four daughters, continue to serve as elders to ten grandchildren and are the proud great grandparents of two toddlers. Now, confidently entering their mid to late 80s, the couple has successfully navigated cancer treatments, joint replacements and whatever other obstacles life has decided to throw their way.

Throughout each of my podcast interviews, I always ask each guest to describe their life in three words. While this question is painfully open-ended for some and a delight to answer for others, I have found that the answers to this question deliver a succinct summary for the entirety of the podcast interview, and act as a true window into the hearts of the interviewees.

Marion's three words were: *Die to Self* — drawing upon a realization of our own mortality and on the fact that we must all think of more than ourselves. Her upbringing in a closely-knit family, with the church at the center of her community, instilled her resolve to place her life in the hands of a greater power. One could argue that this is how she has managed to beat cancer and successfully endure multiple joint replacements well into her eighth decade on Earth. To her, "Die to Self" means that, in order to be successful and truly happy, we need to get out of our own way and replace the idea of "self" with a focus on the bigger picture at play.

Mickey's three words were: *I Love Marion*. As he said them, I could see the faint trace of tears beginning to form in his eyes. His voice even narrowed and got a few degrees lower. I could tell that, as he spoke these three words, his mind was replaying decades of memories and emotional dances. His love for his bride and her support throughout all the different seasons of his life and career, are what has allowed him to pursue such a wide range of passions and impact an incredible number of people.

In addition to sharing their personal stories with me, both Marion and Mickey kept coming back to the importance of family and faith in their lives, and how these core values would serve as building blocks for their own perseverance and resilience time and time again.

BRINGING THIS ALL TOGETHER

By now you may be thinking:

Nice stories Myles, but what does this have to do with Unseen Work?

At the beginning of this book, I laid out the three main types of Unseen Work which have become apparent to me after hundreds of podcast interviews. I also introduced this idea that, when leveraged together, our Unseen Work can help us bridge the gap between our perceived and actual realities. I defined the first type of Unseen Work as Generational Unseen Work — the foundation which each of our lives is built upon. Instead of opening this book with stories directly about me, I decided to tell you about my family: these stories are the beginning of my own Generational Unseen Work.

Marion and Mickey are my grandparents.

Their life stories and all of their hard work – both unseen and seen – have laid the foundation for my own pursuits. In fact, Mickey's name is actually Myles. Mickey is a nickname he had when he was younger. I decided to introduce him in this manner as to not add any confusion since we share the same name.

Fun fact – I am the third Myles Joseph in my family. First was Myles Joseph McManus, my Grandfather's uncle. Then my grandfather, Myles Joseph Hergert. And now me, Myles Joseph Biggs. Growing up, my grandfather always made a big deal about this. I have fond memories of him taking me under his wing and somewhat parading me around town on errands: telling everyone who would listen that I am his namesake. For a little kid, that meant a lot. And it still does. I think of those memories with a smile and warmth in my heart. And, in reliving those memories through the lens of Unseen Work, I am confident that sharing a name with my grandfather has influenced the way I see the world, and myself, and has undeniably helped shape my identity from an early age. Without even thinking, I have modeled his behavior as a way to live up to the Myles name.

I was able to capture the stories I just shared with you in August of 2019. I had around two weeks of blissful unemployment as I transitioned out of one job and got ready to begin another. I decided to take this rare opportunity of a professional vacuum to visit my grandparents in New Jersey. I sat across from them at the dining room table, in that house that my grandfather initially built as a summer cottage, asking them questions for over two hours. Thankfully, they agreed to have those conversations recorded and shared with the world on my podcast. It was so much fun and an experience I will forever cherish and be grateful for.

This exercise really got me thinking. Not just about Unseen Work, but about the oddity that can be family. I think it's easy for us to only see familial authority figures in our lives as the embodiment of their authority. A grandparent becomes the title of "grandparent" instead of also being the person which led them to that position of honor. No matter how old you are, you will always be someone's child or grandchild. When they look at you, they will see the child you once were. When you look at them, you will see them for the idol and teacher you had in them throughout your formative years. In many ways, this is as it should be. It's a point of respect. However, because of these notions and somewhat unspoken rules of engagement, we don't always get to fully know the people we love. Family members are quick to say, "I Love You," but not always as quick to truly get to know the person with whom they are exchanging this phrase. By allowing time to pass without these conversations, we lose the opportunity to fully appreciate our own Generational Unseen Work or deepen our existing connections.

A hot topic right now is "finding your why." For me, and probably for most parents, a big driver of everything I do – my "why" – is to set a good example for my children. This reflection on the impact of Generational Unseen Work has led me to the idea of family as a mirror — one generation is a reflection and adaptation of the one before it. I find this to be especially true in my own journey as a father. My son has forced me to see both the good and the bad about myself on a daily basis. As he grows up, I want him to see a father who challenges himself, who rises to the occasion and who does not make excuses for failure, but instead, uses it as fuel for future opportunities. I want him to see someone who doesn't quit. I want him to see life-long learning and someone with a sense of wonder and a thirst for life.

I do not want him to see someone who throws all of their

energy into work and then delivers whatever is left to the family unit at home. I do not want him to see someone who uses alcohol as an escape mechanism or as a way to deal with stress or numb pain. I do not want him to see someone who cannot control their emotions or their words, or someone who acts impulsively and without regard for others.

As mirrors, children reflect what they see, not what we say. This whole line of thought hit home for me one day when my son went into his playroom and picked up a toy plastic chair. He then walked it to the other end of the house, through my bedroom and into the bathroom. Once in the bathroom, he placed it in front of my vanity sink, stepped onto it and then motioned for a toothbrush. I got him the brush and he proceeded to brush his teeth. Stopping every now and then to place his brush under the faucet and (in his own one-and-a-half-year-old words) ask me to turn the water on. I decided to brush my teeth with him since we already had the tooth brushing mood set. When I was done, I stuck my mouth under the stream of water to rinse my mouth. Well, sure enough, here is my little guy trying to pull himself up to do the exact same thing I just did. What he saw me do. Not anything I told him to do.

A mirror. A reflection.

We grow up watching the example set for us by our parents — their actions and their words. Our parents learned their behavior from their parents. And so on. Generational Unseen Work shapes all of us. Even when we say we are not going to act with our children the way our parents acted with us, it's a learned behavior. It's a decision based on unspoken actions of past generations and how we have processed them (in an unseen fashion) in our own heads, forming our thoughts and opinions and skewing the way we approach each and every situation.

CHAPTER 4:
THE P.K.

Singing slightly off key and marching confidently from the front altar to the doorway at the rear of the congregation, the Pastor seemed to smile wider and wider with each booming note and graceful stride. Soon the imposing pipe organ faded into the quiet, yet excited chatter of the churchgoers as everyone filed out from their pews and into the middle aisle. Before exiting the church, each person stopped to shake the Pastor's hand and exchange a few well wishes before returning to the hustle and bustle of daily life.

Smartly dressed and beaming with pride, two young boys stood at the Pastor's side, practicing their very best big-boy handshakes with each member of the congregation. As the Pastor's sons, they were proudly on display at nearly every church function; expected to be on their best behavior and to serve as an extension, not only of their father, but of the church itself.

Growing up as a pastor's kid, or P.K. as those with this status are often referred to, is a special experience akin to having a parent in elected public office or similar position of authority within the community. Often, a pastor's home is directly next to their church. This means that, while most kids only think about church on Sundays or Holidays, a P.K. has church woven into the very fabric of their days. While other kids might be able to fake sick and binge cartoons instead of singing in the choir, the only thing excusing a P.K. from the weekly worship service are serious illnesses requiring hospitalization.

While the church was at the center of his family's daily life, this particular Pastor did not force the idea of following in the family business on his sons. If they had been called to serve God and the Church, he would have certainly been proud, however, it was not his expectation. Instead, he supported both boys' passions whole-heartedly and leveraged the flexibility of his schedule to be sure he attended every baseball game and school activity possible. At home, he purposefully did not bring Church issues to the dinner table or focus on God in every conversation. Instead, he worked to instill Christian values in his boys through his own actions towards others, whether he was at the front altar or in the bleachers cheering for a base hit.

As the boys aged, the eldest son tested his father with a rebellious streak. He and his brother would slide down the middle aisle at church on their knees, bounding around and intent on causing a purposeful ruckus. He built underground forts in the woods to hide out from the spotlight which followed his family, and to plan these stunts and other elaborate pranks. As a child of the 1960s, this time in the woods was spent without cell phones or GPS tracking devices — leaving his parents to rest their faith in God to be sure their son wouldn't get into too much trouble and would return home in time for dinner. Which, he always did. At his heart, he always wanted to please his parents. But, as any child in the public eye can attest to, sometimes being raised by a village can be a bit too much to handle — especially in those formative teenage years.

After completing his schooling with a college degree in psychology, the eldest son went to work for a power utility. A company, uncharacteristically by today's standards, he has been with for over three decades. Throughout his career, he took a shot at being in the spotlight like his father had been, applying for supervisory roles and working to climb the corporate ladder. But he quickly found that he preferred to focus on controlling his own work, rather than having to cater to the variables of direct reports and inter-office politics. He saw his coworkers chase status, position and money only to be metaphorically chained to their desks and miss important moments in their kid's lives. This was not his goal. As his father did before him, he valued the freedom of flexibility in his work so that family functions could come first.

The eldest son went on to marry his college sweetheart and have three children. Just as his father did before him, he grabbed onto that career flexibility with both arms and constantly adjusted his schedule to drive the sports-practice-taxi, attend games, go on scouting trips and be a prominent presence in his children's lives. Also like his father, work was never a topic of dinner table discussion. Instead, he focused on raising his children to talk about the great things that happened each day, what their dreams were and to enjoy the close-knit bond of the daily family dinner and weekly family game nights.

Now, at almost 60 years old, he would tell you that he's in his favorite decade of life, so far. His children are all grown up and out of the house. He's also a new grandfather and is now relishing the joys of having a toddler tackle him and erupt into a fit of giggles. Having raised three, self-sufficient children, his role has moved from an authority figure to friend and he can sit back to enjoy and take pride in his family.

Perhaps passed down to him from his Pastor father, he counts his passion in life as being a cheerleader for others. He makes it a point to tell people they did a good job, or pay them a compliment, or tell them that he's proud of something they have done. His goal is to be a voice for goodness in a world that increasingly focuses on the negative. This brings him joy.

Even though the Pastor has passed on, he would be proud to see that, all these years later, his son continues to live the Christian values. Those lessons taught from as early as he could stand at the back of the church, shake hands and wish others a wonderful day, have lasted a lifetime.

CHAPTER 5:
THE CARING CREATIVE

The excitement in the room was palpable. Attendees alternated between hushed comments and bouts of enthusiastic applause and approving smiles. An outsider could have easily accused every man in attendance of performing their best James Bond impression. Each of them handsomely sporting their very best social regalia. Likewise, the women they were escorting filled every inch of the room with their radiance and elegance. As music began to overpower the conversations within the crowd, a blanket of silence enveloped the attendees.

Visually breaking this silence, a young woman emerged onto a second-story landing and gracefully floated down a palatial spiral staircase. Her father stood patiently and proudly waiting — with an extended arm and an outstretched heart — to escort her into the social fray. As the pair began their slow descent, the young woman was announced by the master of ceremonies; a few onlookers shared approving nods, while others went back to stealing hushed whispers, remarking about the beauty of her dress. As the pair approached the final step, the woman's mother stepped forward with a large bouquet of flowers, presenting them to her daughter along with a gentle kiss on the cheek and a whisper of encouragement in her ear.

Firmly grasping her floral arrangement, the young woman

strode to the dance floor to take her place on the edge of a carefully arranged throne; back skillfully straight, ankles crossed, and neck extended. Perfectly executing the finesse expected for the occasion. Her white gloved hands were folded neatly and fell gracefully to her lap, careful not to bruise the fragile roses still in her grasp. Once the young woman was settled, with her father assuming his protective position behind her chair, the crowd shifted their attention back to the landing at the top of the stairs and the process began once more.

Just now, while your mind may have been conjuring up images of a wedding reception, this was, in fact, a Debutante Ball. These events, sometimes referred to as cotillions, originated in Europe and were a means for young women from prestigious families to be introduced into high society for the first time. As the event has become popularized in the United States, the honor has moved beyond prestigious, in terms of familial status, and now honors women of high standing in their communities based on their academic achievement and philanthropic contributions.

This particular scene was from a Debutante Ball in the 1970s. Back then, young women were selected to apply for the Debutante program in their senior year of high school. As mentioned above, their applications would be judged on levels of community service, performance in school, and on character recommendations from upstanding members of the community. If selected, the women would begin their training. These future Debutantes would attend classes instructing them in how to properly dance the waltz, the correct way to set a table (accounting for each and every size of fork and spoon you can imagine), as well as proper social decorum when attending formal events. Most of all, they would have the opportunity to be praised for their personal accomplishments and to feel like a princess for an evening; making memories with their fathers and mothers which would stay with them well into their adult years.

The young woman highlighted at the onset of this section, would grow up to complete her Bachelor's degree in nursing, earn a Registered Nurse (RN) certification, work for nearly two decades in hospital emergency rooms, and then transition into a second career of nearly two decades as a school nurse.

As a young child, years before her Debutante debut, this young woman would battle her fair share of illnesses; some of which would require hospitalization. While she had a few moments typical of most children, like a broken arm while falling off a bike (which accounted for one of the previously mentioned hospital stays), she also suffered from severe asthma-like symptoms. Today, an illness like asthma is entirely treatable through a mix of inhalers, nebulizer machines and other forms of inhaled steroid treatments. However, as a child growing up in the 1960s and 1970s, an asthma attack would often require hands-on medical care for professionals in a hospital environment.

This time spent around healthcare professionals throughout her formative years no doubt shaped her desire to enter into the nursing profession. In a way, by caring for countless children today — working to soothe their illnesses, both physical ailments and mental anxieties — she is paying forward the care and attention she was given when she was young. She views nursing as a calling.

She also views it as a creative outlet.

It's common for those in the healthcare field to be miscategorized as heavier left-brain users. The left side of our brains not only controls the right side of our body, but also it gets credit for all cognitive functions related to logic, science and mathematics. On the surface, it's easy to make this assumption. The daily duties of nursing do, in fact, require ongoing mental math and knowledge recall of everything from human anatomy to how certain medicines interact with one another. However, if this young woman took anything away from her training as a Debutante, it wasn't the importance of which fork to use with your salad. While at first glance the fine arts of high-society may seem unimportant, those lessons have helped her to navigate the most dangerous variable in medicine.

People.

Whether it's white gloves or a white lab coat, you do not want to underestimate this woman. Her daily work may not be in a formal social setting with rules of engagement and pleasantries to adhere to, but the ability to navigate difficult social situations with confidence and a command of your own emotions is a pivotal component to bedside manner.

As a school nurse, caring for hundreds of children in a disadvantaged urban setting, left-brain logic is absolutely helpful. However, her ability to engage her right-brain, her creative side, and mix of the right concoction of equal parts medical training, powerful conversation, and unbridled confidence in herself, makes her a force to be reckoned with. On any given day, her job will shift from caring for a childhood diabetic or asthmatic, to coaching a parent on the best way to both care for themselves and care for their child.

Now, after giving of herself for years and years, and with retirement slowly coming into view, her children give her strength. Not only her three biological children, but the countless number of children she has provided for in her career as a school nurse. Children who hand-make her postcards to tell her that she is their sunshine or the best nurse they've ever had. Children who come back to her elementary school after entering middle or high school to share with her that the lessons she imparted on them have taken root, and they still draw upon them in their daily lives. These repetitive tugs on her heart strings keep her going. In drawing strength from her, those kids actually provide her with more strength than they could ever imagine.

COLLEGE SWEETHEARTS

It was 1980-something in the cafeteria of Seton Hall University in South Orange, New Jersey. A tall underclassman with shaggy hair and ombre-tinted, aviator-style eyeglasses was commiserating with a group of his friends. He confidently wore powder blue pants and jacket, along with a yellow shirt, which was just a few shades lighter than his sandy hair.

Ladies and gentlemen, the eldest son of the Lutheran Pastor in our previous story, was all grown up.

Across the room, a young woman sat stealing glances at Mr. Powder Blue. Alternating between darting glances and excited chatter among her group of girlfriends. After these periods of momentary slouching, necessary in the art of hushed conversation, her back snapped right back to attention and she remained literally — and in this moment, emotionally — on the edge of her seat. Yes, my friends, you can't quite kick that Debutante schooling.

After months of ogling from a distance and a failed attempt by a mutual friend to set our female character up with the roommate of our shaggy-haired friend, our two love birds finally began dating. A courtship that would last the remainder of their college career and would blossom into a marriage now lasting in excess of three decades.

CHAPTER 6:
GENERATIONAL UNSEEN WORK SUMMARY

Since this section of the book is defined as Generational Unseen Work, and I already spilled the beans about Marion and Myles being my grandparents, it should come as no surprise to learn that the Pastor's son and the nurse in these stories are my own father and mother: David and Kathleen Biggs. To drop another generational knowledge bomb on you all, Kathleen is also the daughter of Marion and Myles.

But, before I go further into unpacking the stories of my parents, I would like to spend a few paragraphs on my father's parents. Unfortunately, MaryLynn and Donald Biggs passed away before I began my interviews. It's something I think about all the time. I truly wish I could have had those one-on-one moments with them and asked the questions I always had in my mind but never got around to asking. So, what follows is some context on the two of them based on what I do know.

THE PASTOR

Donald Biggs grew up in Mobile, Alabama. His father was not much of a role model; he spent much of his time struggling with his own demons and issues with alcohol, leaving him a bit detached from family life during his son's formative years — they would reconnect later in life, however.

Remember the "pastor" character briefly mentioned "The P.K." section above? That was Donald.

At age 16, he went away to the seminary to become a Lutheran pastor. Perhaps it was his lack of a tight-knit family that led him to the Church as a strong foundation, but I will never know for sure. For whatever reason, he spent his entire life leading others in their faith journeys. I can remember as a young boy, taking the spot next to him at the back of church just as my father had done decades earlier, to greet people at the end of a service. It's quite a thing to grow up and see your grandfather, or Papa as I called him, stand up in front of a room of people, preaching and dissecting the complex topics of faith and morality.

For all I learned from him during my formative years while he was alive, I learned the most about my Papa at his funeral. The service was brimming with people from all over the country. As a Pastor, Donald had led congregations in several states, and many of these groups arrived in school busses to be sure they could honor his memory. Countless people came up to me at the service and shared stories with me about how he had helped them through a difficult time, how they loved it when he led the choir with a booming (and sometimes off-key) confidence, and about how he always bragged about me and about his other grandchildren when meeting with members of the church.

Shortly after his funeral, one of the congregations he had previously led, Martini Lutheran Church in Baltimore, Maryland, held an event called Pastor Biggs Sunday. I would learn that they had held this event regularly for years after he had retired. He would make it a point of traveling from his home in Pennsylvania to Maryland to lead a service at least once a year. The congregation invited our entire family to this particular Pastor Biggs Sunday, right after his passing, as an extended memorial service for those who were unable to attend his funeral across state lines. What a humbling experience. Again, more and more people with stories of how he had affected their lives. I thought it was odd that, in the twenty-four years that I had known him, I never heard of this event while my Papa was alive. But, hearing my own father talk about his childhood, I realize now that this was simply how he operated — he had a pretty good separation between his faith-family and his family-family.

Growing up, as it was for my father, it wasn't always easy having a faith leader for a grandparent. It would often feel as though he was preaching to me, his own grandson, rather than simply being a supportive family member. He would force us to sit and read the bible on religious holidays like Christmas or Easter, and there was censorship on TV shows like *Power Rangers* when I was young. But what I now know, unfortunately now that he is gone, is that being a pastor was not a job for him, it was *who he was*. Whether it was leading a service at church or as the patriarch of our own family, he was called to be a voice of moral authority. Because of this, as I mentioned above, his combined family is massive. I have now met dozens of couples he has married, even more that he has baptized, and others who can remember a time when he was there to support them at a very low moment in their journey. Through those interactions, I have gained an acute awareness of where my own father received his personal values and can now realize how important moments with Papa were for me in my own formative years. I'm proud to say I have inherited some of his servant-leader qualities.

A PROUD PASTOR'S WIFE

MaryLynn Biggs is my father's mother and my grandmother, or Nana as we called her. She grew up in Green Bay, Wisconsin and into a family with heavy, German roots. Both of her parents were in the medical field, with her mother working as a nurse and her father as a prominent pathologist and radiologist. Perhaps this is why my father was drawn to my mother, the nursing major. After Nana was born, her mother chose to stay home and focus on raising her instead of continuing in her career. She transitioned into the role of homemaker and "Doctor's Wife." Nana's mother took great joy in hosting dinner parties for doctors and other hospital executives. In watching her mother take great care in entertaining, my Nana grew to mirror that skill. I have many memories of her fussing over tiny event details — down to the color of the plates and napkins on each occasion. This, in her own way, was a means for her to communicate her love for those in attendance.

As a child, her favorite activities tilted in the opposite direction of the medical sciences and included making paper dolls, drawing, painting, and the theater. She met Donald early in her adulthood, when they were both working at a Lutheran summer camp in the Indiana/Illinois region.

Nana was a devoutly religious woman. In many ways, it is fitting that she met her future husband at a church-related event and that he would become a pastor. After they were married, she happily latched on to the identity of "Pastor's Wife." Just as her mother had proudly worn the title of "Doctor's Wife." In fact, when asking my father about Nana, he even joked that the role of "Pastor's Wife" was her longest-running career. She took great joy in working alongside him at the church. In many ways, her role was very similar to that of the First Lady. While Papa was running the business side of the church, Nana was very active in educational programs and community outreach. Throughout her life, she also served in a variety of capacities outside of the church as well, including as a teacher and librarian, and even an associate at the once famed department store, Abraham and Strauss, in their fine china department. Even while fulfilling her main role as a co-head of the church, Nana never stopped pursuing her own passions.

NATURE VS. NURTURE

In listening back to my interviews with my parents and my grandparents (as well as reflecting on my time with the grandparents I was not able to interview) and on my own thirty years on this planet, it's amazing what I have become aware of through these lenses of Generational Unseen Work.

I can see so much of my grandparents — their personality traits, their values, their actions — in my parents. Likewise, as I reflect on my own life, I now notice that I am a true blending of the mindsets, values, and actions of these two generations.

I am the grandson of a carpenter, a politician, an entrepreneur, a salesman, a pastor, a teacher, a businesswoman and several types of community leaders. I am the son of a nurse, an analyst, an artist, and musicians.

Many people make the argument for nature vs. nurture; however, I no longer believe that the two are mutually exclusive. Just as Unseen Work and seen work are not mutually exclusive. As a parent, I now know, with certainty, that we are all born with certain personality traits which are simply hardwired into us. Without being told or taught anything, I've seen my son assert himself or laugh at his own jokes as young as eleven months old. That's nature. However, I'll argue that *nurture* is the lens through which we view our *nature*.

As a child, I grew up watching my Grandfather, Myles, approach strangers and strike up conversations with them, eliciting laughter and smiles from just about everyone he approached. I saw my Papa, Donald, lead a large congregation in prayer and then greet each person by name and engage in real and personalized conversation with every individual.

I watched my Grandma, Marion, turn a haphazard thrift store into a thriving philanthropic enterprise. I watched my Nana, MaryLynn, transform a sterile church all-purpose room into a warm and inviting community space.

I watched my Father, David, work long hours to provide for his family but never once show an ounce of stress or voice a single complaint — showing up and smiling for every one of our childhood activities. I watched my Mom, Kathleen, run from the house in her nightgown and hair curlers to help a neighborhood child who had fallen off his bike in the middle of the road — not giving a damn about her own appearance, only focused on how she could help someone in need.

This is just what I saw. Or overheard. I can only imagine what I have not been able to witness.

Each of these instances of seen work, by my generational predecessors, has fueled my personal Unseen Work and tinted the lens through which I have interpreted my own personality traits, my thoughts, and my value system. Not to mention my view of others in this world.

I believe that this Generational Unseen Work begins playing a role in the nurturing of our nature before we are young enough to remember their affect.

Let's continue to use me as an example.

When I was 18 years old, I attained the rank of Eagle Scout. Did I work hard for it? You're damn right I did! However, part of what kept driving me toward the goal, even when I wanted to quit, was a small phrase I once overheard my Grandfather, Myles, say when discussing my Boy Scout career with my parents. He shared how happy he was to see me enjoying Scouts and that he had made it to the rank of Life Scout (the rank just before Eagle Scout) and then his life took over.

Remember, this was the man who left high school a year early to begin work as a carpenter as a way to help provide for his family of twelve people.

The mere fact that I was even able to enjoy a full 18 years as a child, and not as a member of the workforce, was due, in part, to the sacrifices he made, and those which other members of my family made, that I will never be able to see. Hearing him mention this small line about life taking over, and almost hinting at it as if he regretted not getting his Eagle, drove me to continue. At my award ceremony, I was able to award someone who had helped me on my journey with a mentor pin — a gold replica of the Eagle Scout badge, in lapel pin form. There were many people I counted as mentors along that journey, including (and especially) my own father, who was right beside me for every camping trip and drove me to nearly every meeting. But when the time came, there was no doubt who would get that pin. When my grandfather accepted it at the ceremony, he turned and faced the crowd with a massive smile. He gave a cheeky bow, held it up in the air and referenced that, it may have taken him several decades, but he had finally gotten his own Eagle. I'll never forget the look on his face.

In my professional career, I have had the opportunity to hold some high-level management positions; charged with overseeing large numbers of people and expected to have a calm head when others often feel tempted to jump from fire to fire. I can remember going to work at the thrift shop with my Grandma, Marion, as a young boy. In her role, she would shepherd a mix of community volunteers and executives within the hospital system her store was supporting. There would be times I could overhear tense phone conversations or watch as someone presented what they viewed as a sky-is-falling problem to my grandma. I always remember her handling it with a smile and a graceful, yet tactical response. She has always had a way to politely challenge and disarm the status quo. I realize now that I have unknowingly channeled her experience on countless occasions.

Public speaking has never been an issue for me. As a student, I was always quick to raise my hand and participate. I held leadership offices in Boy Scouts, was the captain of sports teams, ran for student government positions, and more. I have also organized a few charitable events which have raised money for cancer research and other notable causes. I'm not saying this to brag about me. This comes from my Papa, Donald and my Nana, MaryLynn, whom I grew up watching step into community leadership roles, seemingly without a second thought. They were always quick to sacrifice their own personal time to improve a personal moment for someone else — even strangers. So, growing up, it was easy for me to do the same. That's just what it meant to be a Biggs.

I do not back down. In college, my reputation bordered on infamy. There was a true dichotomy of life-long friendships formed, and arch enemies created. At times, my confidence did (and still can) creep into arrogance. I'll own that, one hundred percent. When I am passionate about something, I feel compelled to stand up and speak my piece.

Thanks, Mom.

Growing up I often heard my Mother, Kathleen, use the term "Kathie Letter" to describe a strongly worded exchange. These were the days before Yelp and online reviews. If you had a negative experience or felt you had been wronged, one of your few choices would be to write that feedback and send it off via regular mail. I know now, that watching my Mom stand up for herself when I was a kid, set the example for me to feel comfortable doing the same.

I can remember my father waking up with me before 5:00 a.m. to be sure I was up and ready to leave the house. Then, he would drive me to my morning swim team practice, two days a week during my sophomore and junior years of high school. Since I could not yet drive, he made sure I got there. He also drove me and picked me up from some of my first dates with my very first girlfriends and dropped me off at friend's houses whenever I needed a lift – the list could go on and on. Even earlier, he volunteered to be an assistant coach for my baseball teams and would sit and listen to me literally cry over striking out again, without issuing judgement. He was just there. All. The. Time. My dad somehow figured out how to manage the societal expectations of being the manly man, working long hours to provide for our family, being the stern disciplinarian, chopping firewood, fixing things around the house – you get the idea – with the less widely acclaimed manly virtues of compassion and empathy. I have vivid memories of all of those things. But, as a new father myself, I realize the greatest present he ever gave me was his presence. It is this Generational Unseen Work that my children will not see when they look at me, but will feel as a result of my own actions. I will know that my ability to be a kind and understanding role model came from my father.

Thanks, Dad.

While this walk down memory lane has been a blast for me to write, some of you may still be scratching your head and wondering how all this applies to you. So, let's go there.

Generational Unseen Work, at its heart, does not mean that no one ever noticed, praised, or simply saw your parents, grandparents, great grandparents, and beyond. It means that when people look at you, what they do not see are the people who stand behind you. Meaning, that part of our Unseen Work, is the seen work of our ancestors. And, cyclically, that means that our accomplishments, our seen work, will be part of our children's Unseen Work. Another commonly used word for this idea is Legacy.

An awareness of, and appreciation for, your own Generational Unseen Work, will help you unlock a new level of self-confidence that can help propel you towards your present-day ambitions. I know this, because it has had that effect for me.

I've developed the following prompts to help guide you through this process. How you use them is up to you. These can be great questions to journal on, allowing you to work through your responses through the free flowing art of writing; you can record yourself asking these questions, and then close your eyes and settle into a mindfulness exercise, allowing yourself to reach a point of stillness and journey back into your subconscious to see the effect of Generational Unseen Work in your mind's eye; and, you could use these questions as a rubric for an in-person interview, sitting down with the elder members of your family and allowing them to share their stories with you one-on-one, giving you both the opportunity to share a moment of connection and personal growth.

Personally, I recommend a mix of all three. In my life, I stumbled through this process unknowingly, and in the reverse order of the way I have presented the three options above. I sat down with family members and interviewed them for my podcast, then found myself thinking about their stories all the time, in an annoying sort of subconscious meditation. Through the process of this book, I have journaled through my feelings on their stories and spent the time needed to arrive at some formative conclusions. I hope that you can learn from my messy process of self-discovery and develop a system that works for you.

GENERATIONAL UNSEEN PROMPTS:

1. What were my parents/grandparents like as kids?
   a. What were their hobbies?
   b. What did they want to be when they grew up?
   c. What are their memories of their parents?
   d. What are their favorite memories of childhood?
   e. What would they describe as some of the most formative moments of their youth — moments that shaped them into who they are today?
2. What are my earliest memories of my parents/grandparents?
   a. Are they positive or negative?
   b. How have they changed the way I see the world?
   c. Do I like the effect they have had on me?
   d. Have I lived my life to please them or to rebel against them?
3. What role has family played in my life?
   a. Which family member did I look up to the most?
      i. Why?
   b. Which family member did I shy away from the most?
      i. Why?
   c. What did I love about family as a kid?
   d. What did I dislike about family as a kid?
4. If/When my own children grow up, what do I want them to remember about me?
   a. What values do I want to pass on?

b. What do I want to do differently than my parents/grandparents?
c. What do I want to do the same as my parents/grandparents?
d. What do I want to be different about the world because my children were in it?

You will notice that not all of these prompts are positive. That's because sometimes the biggest lessons we learn from family members are what, and who, we do not want to be. Earlier, I initiated the idea of children as mirrors, reflecting our own actions. But, when we look in the mirror and don't like what we see, we make a change — altering our clothes, our hair, a facial expression – you get the idea. As much as we unconditionally love the generations, which came before us, sometimes they can be a stark reminder of what we don't want to become ourselves. This is why you hear people grumble about family coming to visit or hosting a big holiday gathering. It forces them to see that reflection they've been working to change.

But, instead of running away or ignoring those whom we do not want to be, a better habit is to embrace where we came from and how we got to our current place in time. By leaning into this way of thinking, we can make sure that we actively achieve the results that we want for ourselves, instead of unknowingly repeating a generational cycle of behavior.

By mastering your appreciation for, and awareness of, Generational Unseen Work in your own life, you'll be best prepared to take advantage of our next topic: Active Unseen Work.

NOTE: You don't have to sort through these prompts alone! Head over to www.mylesbiggs.com for information on the Unseen Work Mastermind. You can request more information, join the waiting list, and get access to a community of like-minded people who are putting in their Unseen Work – just like you.

PART 2:
ACTIVE UNSEEN WORK

CHAPTER 7:
THE FUTURE MOGUL

After turning off 8th Street and onto Hennepin Avenue, there was no way you could miss it – a crimson landing strip beckoning the movers and shakers of Minneapolis to the entrance of Seven Steakhouse. Here, the event's host was waiting. As guests strolled the red carpet, posing for photos and brimming with anticipation, he was all business.

If this was a traditional corporate networking event, his ripped skinny jeans, backwards ballcap and 1995 birthdate might expose him as an outsider instead of a visionary – a title, which success after success had rightfully been bestowed upon him, regardless of appearance or age. As the event's final touches came to a close, he moved methodically about the space, relaying commands to his team with intensity but not arrogance. Each request was fulfilled without hesitation; their respect for him evident through their actions.

As guests began to filter into the room, his attention shifted seamlessly from preparation to politicking – shaking hands, exchanging smiles, and welcoming a majority of attendees by their first name. The clock struck 6:00 p.m. and with swift obedience, the crowd fell silent upon his command. Recently voted to be the year's Young Entrepreneur of the Year for the entire state of Minnesota, he was no stranger to the spotlight. But his journey to this moment began years prior, and it was not always marked by confidence. This "overnight success," as some have described it, has been the product of many sleepless nights.

Meet Brandon Poliszuk.

As a child, this would-be entrepreneur could be found comfortably hugging the back corner of the room; purposefully avoiding attention. While his fellow classmates volleyed back and forth for validation and chasing opportunities for attention, Brandon spent more time in his own head than in front of a crowd. While other kids couldn't wait to shoot a confident hand into the air to show off their knowledge, Brandon's hand remained glued to his desk. The opposite of confident, he was always second guessing his own thoughts and worrying about how the world would see him.

So, how did Brandon transform himself from meek and mild to extraverted and entrepreneurial?

At 18 years old, he took a job selling fiber-optic internet and cable door-to-door. He would be dropped off in affluent neighborhoods and was required to make trips to each house at three different times in order to maximize the chances of speaking with someone. In his words, he got his "face kicked in" over 100 times a day with varying degrees of rejection. But rather than focusing on the negative, he continued to pursue the sale. The job was commission-only but paid him 100% of what he sold. So, he started the numbers game, sifting through piles of *no's* until receiving an exhilarating *yes*. This taught him persistence, how to separate his own personal identity from professional setbacks, and the value of action.

His next job was at PAC Sun, selling clothes. Armed with his newly forged armor against crushing rejection, he set out to approach every single person who entered the store. Here, he learned how to relate to people through the art of conversation. Instead of nagging every customer with a canned sales pitch of "buy one get one half off" he would engage with them, as human beings. He learned that if he could find some way to connect with them or compliment a piece of clothing they were already wearing; he had a higher success rate in selling them additional pieces. He did so well that he was on the path to store management but opted instead to pursue higher education.

In college, he saw an ad on a campus bulletin board for an independent sales representative. It didn't matter that he had never sold newspaper ads before. He figured that if he could peddle internet and phone bundles to stay-at-home moms, or ripped jeans to teenagers, connecting the campus newspaper to area businesses would be par for the course. He wasn't wrong. His customers loved him. They just didn't love the product. This isn't 1990, after all, and businesses near his school knew that the best way to reach their audience would be through smartphones and social networks.

The timing was serendipitous.

In one of his business classes, Brandon's professor was challenging students to create "fake" businesses as a way to better understand the business plan writing process. Brandon took this opportunity to one-up the assignment and create an actual business. He had already formed relationships with area businesses, he knew how to sell, and he was no stranger to overcoming rejection – now he just needed to create a product that would sell.

It started simple. Facebook ads for hire. He aggregated content that was already created and catered the messaging to the college student demographic. It worked. He was selling content packages to clients left and right. But Brandon knew that if he was going to set himself apart, it wouldn't be enough to simply repackage content from other people, he would have to create his own.

He walked into an electronics store with a budget of $500 and walked out $1,400 in credit card debt. The proud owner of a new camera that he did not even know how to turn on.

The Social Butterfly Company was born.

They say that *necessity* is the mother of invention. This is completely true. In Brandon's case, and for many other entrepreneurs, we can add to the idea that *debt* might be known as the crazy uncle and *impatience* as a second cousin.

Knowing he had just put himself in debt and did not actually have the money to pay the credit card bill which would be arriving in a month, Brandon got to work. He sat on YouTube for seemingly endless stretches of time, eating up every tutorial possible. He enlisted his friends to star in poorly made movies so that he could test his developing director skills. This cycle continued for the rest of his college career: selling local social ads, creating content at an increasingly higher proficiency rate, using that content to pump up his brand, sell more ads, and so on. By the time he graduated, Brandon had emerged from his childhood cocoon of self-doubt and entered the world as a confident and calculated small business owner.

He started recruiting other college-aged creators like himself and building out his team. They moved from his dorm room to a coffee shop. Then from a rundown office and into a modern suite in an updated building and most recently into their very own location. His clients have transitioned from local mom and pop pizza shops touting dollar slices to the Minnesota Vikings and multi-millionaire, LA-based influencers.

When asked to describe the journey into business so far, Brandon replied firmly:

"I'm not done."

At 23 years old, I believe him. Can you imagine where he will be in another twenty-three?

TAKEAWAYS

The beginning of this feature on Brandon was not fiction, nor was it exaggerated for storytelling purposes. I witnessed it firsthand when I flew from Pennsylvania to Minneapolis for the sixth installment of his networking event: Link 'N Drink. It was the first time I met Brandon in person, and he lived up to his on-phone and online personality, one hundred percent.

Ironically, this in-person meeting was also the culmination of some Active Unseen Work of my own. In the early days of my podcast, I reached out for advice from other people with different types of online shows as a way to fast track my own knowledge base. I also reached out to fellow podcasters in hopes that they would join me on my podcast and that I could be on their show in return, for a bit of mutual promotion in the name of audience promotion. One of the podcasts that granted me some nuggets of wisdom was The Backpocket Podcast, hosted by Andrew Inserra and Declan Brown, based in Minneapolis, Minnesota. Another Minneapolis-based podcaster, Tyler Webb, had me as a guest in the early days of his show, the How They're Here podcast. In the wake of these two digital interactions, we all followed each other on social media. The initial contact I had with these three people led to a slew of additional podcast episodes featuring people from the Twin Cities — including Brandon. I ended up with so much Minneapolis-based content that when I finally flew out to meet everyone in person, after over a year of online interactions, some people in the city actually thought I was based in Minnesota. My purposeful steps toward growing an online audience eventually led to some awesome, real-world friendships.

There were hundreds of people at Link 'N Drink, and Brandon moved gracefully through the crowd to interact with all of them — myself included! There was no hope of my flying under the radar as Brandon told anyone in my vicinity about how I had flown from Pennsylvania to Minneapolis just for the event. He had even given me personal shoutouts from his company social profiles to let everyone know I would be there. He didn't have to do that. But I can sense from him that he loves it when people claw their way into the spotlight — just like he had to do.

When the night was over, a receiving line formed that would envy the most extravagant of weddings. Brandon personally said goodbye to, hugged, and fist-bumped each attendee. As I waited in line for my turn, I could also hear him asking each person what they thought of the event, if they had fun, and what they could do to make the event better next time. You just can't fake that authenticity.

For me, Brandon's story is another challenge of the age-old argument of nature vs. nurture. Here is a guy who grew up shy and introverted and, through consistent and disciplined work on himself, has emerged as a *social butterfly*.

Brandon's method for accomplishing this transformation can be summarized into one of his favorite sayings: fail fast and fail often. Even more than that, he can look back at failures and learn from them; finding a way to use them in his next attempts at success.

Yes, that may sound cliché, but let's break this idea down in the context of Brandon to prove its meaning beyond an over-used phrase.

Fail fast and fail often means you must take action. That's at the heart of Active Unseen Work. When you want a goal or lifestyle that is far off in the distance, the only way to get there is by starting. In Brandon's case, as he grows his core business and branches off into side projects, he's repeating what he learned as a teenager. To this day, he uses what he learned ringing doorbells in the hopes of earning 100% commission on internet packages. He strikes up conversations using the value-add formula he cultivated while upselling shoppers at PAC Sun. To us outsiders, this seems effortless, but only Brandon knows the complex, experience-based calculus happening in his head during each of these situations.

If you search for Brandon's work on YouTube, you'll still find his first videos. Videos that, in his words, are shitty. Because he believes that you have to put out the shitty video. You have to show people where you came from, and you have to *remind yourself* where you came from. The shittier videos you put out, the more feedback you get, and the better you get.

If you're not obsessed with moving forward, with getting better, then you are approaching average. For some people, being average is OK. Not for Brandon. In our one-on-one conversations, he has told me that the harder he works the luckier he gets. The luckier he gets the harder, and smarter, he has to work. Ultimately, you don't get what you don't ask for. You don't ask for what you feel you don't deserve. That's some insight into the cycle of self-talk that happens in his mind every day.

How do you get to this point yourself? You work for it.

Brandon is at a point now where almost all of his work is seen. He's positioned himself firmly in the spotlight. However, no one can see what's in his head. This is the Unseen Work he puts in every day. As the man at the helm of his business, responsible for a team of people he has personally hired, he constantly experiences the highs and lows of entrepreneurship. Some days he's at the top of the world, and other days he's wondering if he'd be happy being someone else's number two. But, to keep his head in the right place, he focuses on feeding his mind. He's always posting new books he's reading and recommending to his Instagram stories. He focuses on keeping his body in shape through workouts and eating clean — again, all documented on social media.

In a way, Brandon has found that by making his Unseen Work, seen, he can harness that accountability and use it to fuel his efforts. In some ways, it can be harder to maintain a position in the spotlight than it is to initially enter into it. When no one knows who you are, your failures remain invisible and they remain your own. However, as a business owner and online influencer, Brandon's failures reflect on his brand and on his team. But, by never losing his underdog mindset, Brandon is sure to not have any failures. Only setbacks. These setbacks are the one-step-back after two-steps forward. They may cause him to pause, but not to stop. Setbacks only become failures when we lose sight of moving forward and allow them to cause a full-stop. When we stop learning from mistakes, that's the failure. And as Brandon told us earlier — he's not done.

CHAPTER 8:
SWIMMING WITH THE SHARKS

In front of them, two imposing wooden doors creep open at a painfully slow pace. Adding to the drama, massive stage lights increase in intensity until their beams feel like rays from an angry sun. As the two contestants walk forward to the beat of a cheesy, network theme song, five celebrity judges eagerly await their presentation. The contestants reach their mark, a producer signals them to begin from beyond the frame, and the words "Hi, Sharks," break the silence. What follows is a passionate proposal and debate, lasting more than an hour — even though viewers of the show see maybe twenty minutes of the back and forth. After the gauntlet of business acumen concludes, the two contestants can be seen accepting a deal from the infamous "shark," Mark Cuban.

Allow me to introduce Sarah Nuse: *Shark Tank* alumnus, wife, mother, business owner, published author, podcast host and accountability coach. While Sarah will list wife and mother as her favorite of those jobs, her business, Tippi Toes Dance Company, is what led her to the *Shark Tank* floor. And, while her appearance on the show concluded with a deal from Mark Cuban, she actually said "no" to Cuban in the months after recording — citing a misalignment of personalities and vision for dissolving the fledgling partnership.

How does an entrepreneur claw their way onto *Shark Tank* and then have the confidence and poise to refuse an already-accepted offer from one of the show's most influential hosts?

You guessed it — Unseen Work.

As a kid, Sarah was a terrible student. Her words, not mine. She just did not have the patience for book knowledge and always found herself itching to take action rather than notes. So much so, that at 12 years old, instead of opening the cliché kid's lemonade stand, she began hosting dance classes in her family's front yard. While her passion had taken root at that young age, her business was not officially born until she was eighteen. Like most great ideas, it was born out of desperation.

In a twist of fate, Sarah found herself juggling two, big life moments: a brand-new car payment and unemployment. So, she went back to what she knew. Dance. She conjured up the skills honed on her family's front lawn and began teaching dance classes at a local daycare to cover her bills. Sarah immediately fell in love with the idea of making dance her career. But, like many dreams, it was put on hold to pursue higher education.

As a fresh, University of Oklahoma graduate, Sarah began the requisite entry-level corporate internship. Of all the things she learned, the most important was the fact that she cannot stand working in an office. Her parents and friends thought she was crazy, but Sarah quit her job, joined forces with her sister and began Tippi Toes Dance Company. To keep costs down, her business model ingeniously took dance to where kids already were — schools, daycares, etc. — freeing up capital that would otherwise go into brick and mortar locations to invest in other areas of the business.

These investments brought us the company mascot, Tippi the Turtle, original music tracks and albums which now serve as the soundtrack for the company's dance classes and have graced the *Billboard* charts, and even Tippi Toes original ballet slippers.

When their idea to turn Tippi the Turtle into a branded TV

show failed, Sarah and her sister found themselves moping around a California hotel room contemplating their next move. At that moment, someone suggested franchising as an off-the-cuff suggestion and the duo took the idea and ran with it. They poured countless hours of energy into building the franchise model; only then realizing how smart some of their past decisions had been. With no need for a physical dance studio, already in possession of a strong brand in their mascot and consistent music and messaging from their endeavors into songwriting — Tippi Toes Dance Company was a prime candidate for franchise opportunities. Better yet, their target market was women just like them — young, creative, and driven women determined to escape the clutches of Corporate America, as well as working moms yearning for more control over their schedules and time with their kids. It's no wonder the Sharks fell in love with the idea!

Sarah has been at the helm of Tippi Toes for over two decades now and has been selling franchise opportunities for just over ten years. In 2020 the company became a global enterprise, opening a franchise in Beijing. Her experiences growing and scaling a global company, along with her interactions with energized and powerful franchise owners, have helped fuel Sarah's side projects of podcasting, book writing, and accountability coaching.

Her podcast, *Destined for Greatness*, highlights guests who have tapped into their inner greatness and are pursuing their dreams and ambitions. She co-hosts this show with her husband Adam, allowing her to pursue her professional passions while still carving out time to balance her relationship with her spouse. Fittingly, several Tippi Toes franchise owners have been guests on the podcast. Also, fittingly, her ability to train, motivate and coach her franchise owners, allowed her to spin off her talents into yet another side business.

The program she began using to onboard her franchisees is now open to the public on a limited basis. In this capacity as an accountability coach, Sarah helps women from all walks of life realize their inner greatness. She works with her clients to track every moment of their day. This works in a few different ways.

Think you don't have enough time to pursue that big goal of yours? Sarah's tracking exercise will make it painstakingly clear how much you value Netflix over your own self-improvement. Also, these time sheets are submitted to Sarah. So, if you tell her you're going to be at the gym at 6:00 a.m. in the morning, she might text you and ask for a picture as proof. Most of the time we're just fine with disappointing ourselves and comfortable rationalizing things away, but when you know someone else is expecting you to come through, it's harder to slack off. From time to time, Sarah notes that people find the program too grueling. But you can't make someone else want something for themselves. The group only works if the participants put in the effort.

Next logical step? A book! After years of collecting research and documenting thousands of interpersonal interactions, Sarah's book, *Destined for Greatness: Living an inspired life from head to Tippi Toes*, synthesizes her main takeaways from life as an entrepreneur into five main areas:

1. Know what you want.
2. Surround yourself with good people.
3. Be good every day and make small deposits consistently.
4. Find out what is blocking your view.
5. Take action.

These five elements hold enormous truths. At the heart of it all, if we do not know where we are going, we will never get there. Likewise, if we are not surrounded by people who support us, what should be easy will be extremely difficult. We only have to be *good* every day and not *great* – it is important not to put undue pressure on ourselves. If we focus on how to make small, but consistent, deposits into our own personal wellness banks, amazing transformations are possible. Just as we need to know where we are going, we also need to know what stands in our way so that we can overcome the obstacle. Finally, her fifth and perhaps most impactful point: take action. Nothing happens without action. We can read every book on self-mastery, develop the most intricate strategies and accountability practices, and develop the most support networks, but if we do not put in the work – if we do not take action – change will not happen.

TAKEAWAYS

Sarah Nuse is, perhaps, the Queen of Active Unseen Work. It should be noted that her tenacity in business is also matched by her personal taste for perseverance. For some people like Sarah, this laser focus comes naturally. As an example, between setting up dance classes in her front yard at age 12 and taking the entrepreneurial plunge with Tippi Toes after college, as a freshman in high school, Sarah joined the tennis team and began playing the sport competitively for the first time. By her junior year, she was a state champion. Let me say that again: *state champion.* That accomplishment did not happen without significant dedication, practice, acceptance of coaching, or an unwavering mental fortitude – skills which continue to boost her career and personal life.

Sarah's Active Unseen Work in business began immediately after identifying her passion for bringing dance to children. This initiated a ripple effect focused on laying the groundwork necessary to meet her minimum personal financial needs. Once Sarah knew she could pay rent and put food on the table, she went all in on expanding her platform. The result has been a cross-functional powerhouse of businesses, all supporting her initial mission in a complementary fashion. While many people experience burnout after adding new ventures to their already packed personal lives, she has found a way to take everything in stride. In the podcast we did together, she introduced me to a mental game she plays with herself as a way to keep her priorities in check.

According to Sarah, in life, we all have rubber balls and glass balls that we must juggle. Our glass balls are things we take extreme care of and cannot allow to drop; because, if we do, they will shatter. Our rubber balls are things that seem important, but if we set them aside, they will continue to bounce in place until we're ready to pick them up again. Knowing the difference makes it simple to keep priorities in check. Glass balls for Sarah are her faith, family, and friendships. Her rubber balls are things like getting the laundry done, taking a trip, doing the dishes, etc. If she has the choice between having a spotless house or spending time with her kids, you won't find her at the kitchen sink.

One of the things she said that still sticks with me is that she isn't trying to raise perfect kids, she's trying to raise amazing adults. I think it's this shift in mindset that allows her to be amazingly successful, but also grounded. Since she manages her time well and gives proper credence to the right priorities, it does not feel like juggling to her. This should be a lesson to the rest of us. If our lives feel like a circus act, we're most likely prioritizing our rubber balls first and then frantically try to keep our glass balls from shattering.

She personifies this focus on priorities with another amazing one liner:

"Be fast with tasks and slow with people."

If we go slow and build lasting relationships with the people in our lives, then the tasks will find a way to take care of themselves, and we won't have to tackle them all alone.

We spent quite some time discussing this mindset and how our ideologies align. Her podcast is called *Destined for Greatness* and mine is called *Relish The Journey*. Each of our podcasts centers on the fact that every single person has greatness inside of them and stories worth telling and sharing. During our back and forth, she mentioned that she believes that the destination really is in the journey. In working towards our goal, we achieve what we really set out to: whether we actually reach the end or not. This idea can be hard for people to stomach. But it's completely true. If we were to instantly attain everything we wanted, it would not have the same impact. This is why lottery winners notoriously go bankrupt shortly after winning. The reward is not in finally reaching that next chapter but in the daily minutes spent bettering ourselves to become worthy of the ending. That is Active Unseen Work.

Where most people are frightened at the idea of the unknown, Sarah is a perfect example of how consistent action can compound into unfathomable results. We can all "what if" ourselves to death, but awesome ideas mean nothing unless we do something with them. When people ask me for advice on starting a business venture, the advice is simple. Start. Take that first step. Begin the glorious Unseen Work that only you will be able to truly appreciate.

During our podcast interview, Sarah put her own twist on my advice of "start," she pointed out that you can always go back to what you are doing at this very moment, but you can never go to a future you have not created yet. Let that sink in:

You can always go back to what you are doing at this very moment, but you can never go to a future you have not yet created.

In this way, the most celebrated piece of Active Unseen Work is the first step you take towards your future creation. It's in choosing to intentionally begin turning your thoughts into action.

CHAPTER 9:
IF YOU THINK YOU CAN DO BETTER – DO IT.

Fog hovered dangerously close to the surface of the water. Even heavier in the air was the feeling of anticipation. The coastline was littered with a mix of athletes, onlookers, and members of the media. While there was no official barrier between any of these groups, an unspoken respect was strictly enforced, leaving each of them to their pre-event rituals.

Athletes wriggled and wrestled with their wetsuits and performed their own special mixes of yoga and aerobics in preparation for the feat ahead of them. Onlookers grew roots into their patches of sand with blankets, towels, chairs, and coolers; settling in for what was sure to be an action-packed event. Members of the media moved methodically and silently, each setting up multiple rigs and wielding camera/lens combinations in excess of forty pounds. While they may have been outwardly quiet, their internal voices were relentlessly evaluating weather conditions, changing ocean tides, and dozens of other factors, which could potentially impact their shots.

It was as part of this third group that Willie Martini proudly belonged. In the midst of this coordinated chaos, he paused for a purposeful moment and inhaled the fog as deeply as he could. This moment was a decade in the making and the product of countless hours of Unseen Work. His heart swelled with gratefulness. This would be a day he would never forget.

As he exhaled one more time, it was if his breath, and not the powerful gusts of wind, became the force sending ripples into the promotional flag above his head. No matter how thick the fog, people across the world could pick that logo out anywhere. After this event he would be able to feature it prominently on his resume — Red Bull.

Rewind the clock ten years from that moment and a much younger Willie Martini could be seen confidently striding across a stage to collect his college diploma. As a newly minted graphic design graduate, he went to work in photo editing for a publication which featured a vast array of outdoor action sports. After a few years of the editing grind, Willie began to notice the need to fix the same sort of mistakes over and over in his edits. One day, after editing the same error for what felt like the one hundredth time, he made a simple, yet life-altering, decision. He could take better photos. And he was going to prove it.

He quit his job, stepped out from behind the computer and founded Willie Martini Photography.

This decision, born of a potent blend of sheer bravado and naivety, quickly gave way to a realization that capturing the perfect photo is much harder than meets the eye. As Willie worked to hone his craft, he bounced back and forth between corporate jobs and making a run at photography full-time. He constantly battled rejection, feeling like his photos were horrible, and an extreme lack of knowledge in marketing and how to both run and scale a business.

But for all of his shortcomings, Willie also learned how to leverage his greatest strength, the original form of social networking, face-to-face communication.

While some people choose to learn new skills in isolation — laboring away in a vacuum of sheer uncertainty — Willie put himself out there. Even though he was barely scraping enough money together to cover day-to-day living expenses, he prioritized investments into his passion. He flew across the country to put himself in the same room with people who excelled at the skills he was learning. He figured that if he could put himself directly in front of his idols, things would start to happen. Willie racked up thousands of air miles attending industry trade shows, photography workshops, off-site mastermind groups, and in-depth portfolio reviews. All the while collecting feedback on his work to further hone his skills and curating genuine relationships with power players in the industry who were capable of fast-tracking his ambitions.

This focus on interpersonal relationships has paid huge dividends for Willie. He was able to score his first paid photoshoot through one such relationship. As a result of befriending the ownership of the climbing gym he belonged to, and building up their trust in him as a person, when the company broke ground on a new exercise facility and needed promotional images, Willie was their first call.

On another occasion, when Willie flew from his home in California to Wyoming to attend a photography workshop, he quickly found out that one of the instructors was a photo editor for Red Bull. Willie approached him, not as a fanboy or salesman, but as a human being. As a fellow artist. He took a genuine interest in him, got to know him throughout the event and built up a solid working relationship for the duration of the event. When he returned home, Willie sent a simple email thanking him for all the insights he provided at the workshop. At the end of the email, he added that if he ever needed help for Red Bull events in California, Willie would love to work with him one day.

Months went by with no response to that email. Then, ironically, in the middle of a week-long photo shoot for *Rock and Ice* magazine, which up to this point had been Willie's biggest opportunity, he received a call from Red Bull asking if he could fill a last minute cancellation at an event in California – *the next day*.

Willie didn't think twice. He finished his job for the magazine early, left on a plane the next day way before dawn. Shot for Red

Bull all day and then edited all night. When he uploaded his final shots to their cloud-based photography system, not only was Willie mentally drained, but his face was exhausted from smiling so much. *He felt lucky to be this tired.* It took years of relentless and grueling Unseen Work, but he was making his dream come true.

A few months after completing his gig with Red Bull, photos that Willie took for the *Heavy Water* event – a highlighted race on the professional Standup Paddleboard circuit – appeared on the cover of *Standup Journal*. I will never forget the phone call I shared with Willie when he told me this news. While he, of course, dreamed that one day his work would be featured on the front cover of a magazine, when the moment arrived, he was not quite prepared for the range of emotions he experienced. Thousands of people have seen, and will see, that magazine cover. Only Willie truly knows the full amount of Unseen Work that went into creating the moment when it was captured.

TAKEAWAYS

When you develop a true passion for something, that love for the hustle and grind carries you through the hardest of times. While most people would have quit after one year of minimal success, Willie stuck it out for nine more years before landing one of his dream clients. Nine more! Now that he' has done it, Willie knows he can do it and is focused on doing it again. He hasn't grown complacent at all. If anything, he is working harder now than ever before. This excerpt from a post on his website sums up Willie's mindset best:

"There's nothing I enjoy more in photography than working with adventure and action sports athletes. As someone who's been involved with action/adventure sports from a young age, it's where I feel the most like myself. I've tailored my life from a young age to incorporate adrenaline inducing, nature inspired sports that connect us with the elements. There are a lot of parallels between top-level athletes and photographers like myself. We have to be as close as we can to the level

these athletes are operating at so that we can put ourselves in the same environments and come away with images that show off the profound physical abilities these folks demonstrate."

When I read those words from Willie, for me, the most impactful idea is the fact that he has "tailored his life" to align with this passion. His brand of photography is not something he simply dabbles in. It has become his lifestyle. This ability to go all-in, in every aspect of his life, is what has fueled, and will continue to fuel, Willie's success.

In many ways, seeing the results of your Unseen Work come together can elicit an intense adrenaline rush akin to what Willie experiences in his life of action sports. An example that may be more universally relatable is winning a game of blackjack. As players gamble and watch their chip counts rise and fall, no matter how strong their poker face, their stomach is in knots. But, when they hit that big payout, no one is fully capable of holding back the sensations of pure unadulterated emotion.

Often, the pursuit of our passions results in more of the stomach-in-knots moments then fist-pumping-in-the-air moments. It's going to be a struggle until you realize that you cannot do it alone. One of my favorite sayings is that your network is your net worth. This is where Willie truly excelled.

So, while Willie was still building his skills as a photographer, more importantly, he was building his rolodex; creating a deep list of names and connections which he could draw upon for support, feedback and opportunity. His commitment to prioritizing networking and mentorship helped to land him in the room with the proper professional connections required to launch the next phase of his career.

It's easy to take for granted Willie's moment on the beach soaking up the glorious site of a Red Bull flag dancing in the wind. But for every minute he stood in that spotlight, there were hundreds of hours spent shooting and editing photos, being turned down by potential clients, losing photo contests, chasing payables, designing a website, figuring out email marketing — the list goes on. Willie will tell you that his business is only about 25% photography. The rest of his time is filled with marketing, billing, and networking. But as Willie puts it, he loves the struggle.

That love for the struggle of being unseen is what primed Willie for that phone call to step onto center stage. It is what will continue to fuel his ability to repeat this success many times over. It's what can fuel your future success as well.

CHAPTER 10:
ACTIVE UNSEEN WORK SUMMARY

As I said in the beginning, Active Unseen Work is a knowing focus on, and pursuit of, a specific goal. It reinforces the idea that, while we can all learn about something by studying it, we truly learn how to do something by actively doing it. If we can think of Generational Unseen Work as laying the foundation for our opportunities, then we can view Active Unseen Work as how we make use of those opportunities.

Brandon, Sarah and Willie were just three of about fifty examples of Active Unseen Work I could have drawn upon from the stories I have curated as a podcaster. I chose them because, while they certainly have their similarities, they are also distinctly different.

Brandon's Active Unseen Work centered mainly on himself. Amidst the professional accolades and high-profile events surrounding Brandon, his company, and his team, this can be an easy point to overlook. Brandon's nature as a child was introverted and shy. However, at a young age he made the decision that this would not be his nature forever. So, he began the years-long journey of nurturing his growth mindset and on pushing himself beyond the limits of his comfort zone. Brandon shows us that it is not enough to simply put our minds to something. Lots of people out there *think* about starting a business. Many more even claim that they will do it one day. Few actually have the gumption to lay down their credit card, spend money they don't have and then go about the grueling process of teaching themselves a trade. It is all about *action*.

After realizing she was headed down a path she was destined to hate, Sarah Nuse decided to defy conventional wisdom and put her college degree to work teaching toddlers to dance. After years of crafting her business model, branching out into the worlds of music and pitching television shows, not every risk paid off for her. However, when she found herself in the literal, national spotlight, in front of millions on *Shark Tank,* there was nothing those business moguls could ask of her that she was not prepared to answer and answer fiercely. The same fire she showed up with on day one, when she was worried about making her rent and car payments, still shines onto every goal Sarah decides to pursue.

Willie's belief in his dream meant that, even though he was counting pennies to pay bills, he prioritized plane trips to be in the presence of his idols over shallow pursuits in night clubs, living the life twenty-somethings aggrandize on social media. Today, he's looked up to by the next generation of action sports photographers, his work is featured on the covers of magazines, and he's imparting his wisdom gained from clawing to the top with others pursuing a similar path.

The common theme here is determination. In its purest form. However, the motivating factors for each person are entirely their own. While we can read their stories or listen to them share details directly, all we can do is imagine the scenes painted by their words. No matter how vivid they might be, they are only stories. The real work remains invisible.

I am positive that right now, some of you reading this book are already rationalizing why this worked for Brandon, Sarah, or Willie, but it will not work for you. While you respect what they have been able to accomplish and architect for themselves, they remain in a separate class apart from your own. You are saying things like:

Yeah, but they started as "kids" and I'm way older.

Teaching yourself how to take pretty pictures or showing toddlers how to dance is not the same as graduating law school.

They just got lucky. I have tried to start my own business a few times now and it never works out like in these stories. It's just not that easy.

If you're one of these people, I'd like to first thank you for admitting it. You're one of my favorite types of people. You make me smile every day. You'd make Brandon, Sarah and Willie smile too. Because they have been where you are right now. Your innately negative comments will simply remind them of how far they have come and of a world they never wish to return to.

These self-limiting beliefs and realities are simply that — your own creation. They are not actually representative of the real world. As they say, perception is reality. Your perception simply needs to change.

Whoever said that changing yourself is hard was just trying to cushion the blow of a perceived failure later on down the road. Making changes to your own nature, through your own nurturing, is actually quite simple. You just have to decide to do it. YOU have to decide. No one else can do it for you. Reading this book, attending seminars, or hiring mentors – while helpful – will not do it for you. It's making the decision to do what I told you I did in the first pages of this book – erase the stranger staring back at you in the mirror. Take your life back!

This requires taking daily action towards making the change. And, like Brandon did with door-to-door sales, you absolutely will get your face kicked in. A lot. But the difference between those people who leverage Unseen Work, and those people who just remain unseen — is work. You have to do the work. I promise, even though it may start small, if you keep working, it will build and build into amazing results.

Active Unseen Work happens in the years of sleepless nights which compound into an overnight success. It's fueled by passion and desire and a bit of arrogance and foolishness. It's when we disregard what society tells us is possible, destroy our own self-limiting beliefs, and set out to create our own definition of the future.

It doesn't matter how old you are, if you've tried before and failed, or if what you're after has never been done before. It all begins with an awareness of the Unseen Work at play in your life. We all have our own versions of it. We either recognize it and harness it, or we glide along blissfully unaware of our own ignorance and missed opportunities for growth. We can either choose to sit on the couch and think about what's possible, or we can stand up and go out into the world and create what's possible. One invisible step at a time.

ACTIVE UNSEEN WORK PROMPTS:

1. What's your current relationship with Active Unseen Work?
   a. After reading this section, as you reflect on your own life, do you notice how you have put it to use?
   b. Or are you still not convinced in your own ability to change your own course?
2. What's a big goal you have for yourself?
   a. What does life look like once you achieve it?
   b. Who do you have to become in order to make it a reality?
   c. What obstacles will you encounter along the way?
   d. How will it feel when you finally achieve it?
   e. Why do you want to achieve it?
   f. What is motivating you to achieve it?
3. Have you been obsessed with being seen before you're ready?
   a. Instead of focusing on the end result, how could you break your intentions down into smaller, actionable goals?
   b. Why do you want to be seen so badly?
   c. How will you feel if it never happens?

4. What literal things are you doing when no one is watching?
    a. Are you spending all of your free time watching television and playing video games?
    b. Or are you reading books about your passion, studying the most successful people in your field, and opening yourself up to new experiences?

It is not an accident that most of these prompts focus on who you are as a person — not just what it is you are working towards. It is a common misconception that, in order to reach our goals, we have to do nothing but work towards them with every waking moment. You can certainly do that, but chances are you'll end up burnt out and discouraged. You could end up with all the success in the world, and still feel zero fulfillment.

The goal with these journaling exercises, whether you choose to journal, meditate on them, or discuss them with a confidant, is to help you identify not only what you're working towards but *why* you want it so badly. Also, *who* you will have to become in order to achieve it. By focusing inward and on self-transformation, achieving our big goals can become a foregone conclusion. Our outward manifestations are often a result of our internal conversations.

In math, the shortest distance between two points is a straight line. In life, we can fail by following this logical way of thinking. Sometimes we need to go forward, backwards and side-to-side, several times over in order to arrive at our intended destination. When we reach the finish line, we can look back and appreciate how we had to take that non-linear path in order to be ready for what we would find at the end. Contrary to popular belief (and math), sometimes the best path to our goals is not the quickest or the shortest, because we learn the most during our twisted loop of a journey.

By mastering your appreciation for, and awareness of, Active Unseen Work in your own life, you'll be best prepared to take advantage of our next topic: Passive Unseen Work.

NOTE: You don't have to sort through these prompts alone! Head over to www.mylesbiggs.com for information on the Unseen Work Mastermind. You can request more information, join the waiting list, and get access to a community of like-minded people who are putting in their Unseen Work – just like you.

PART 3:
PASSIVE UNSEEN WORK

CHAPTER 11:
THE HITCHHIKER

After loading the bare necessities into his knapsack and catching a train out of town, Yonason Goldson arrived at his first intended location on a hitchhiking trip across the United States, expecting to find a youth hostel in Albuquerque. Instead, upon arriving, a donut shop stared back at him. Suddenly, the confidence and defiance which kicked off his adventure felt more like uncertainty — with a dash of defeat. Forced to improvise, Yonason found a local campground and hastily pitched his one-man pup tent as the sun began to set. As many of us would, he figured a good night's sleep would cure-all and he would be able to re-evaluate his plan the next day. Sleep found him quickly. However, it would be fleeting.

In an instant, the night air shifted from peaceful and still, to violent. The universe seemed intent on testing the young traveler. Yonason woke up to the sensation of his tent collapsing on top of him. In his hurry to end one day and begin the next, he had forgotten to stake out his tent. A rookie move. Now he had to get dressed, run outside, stake down his tent, and then dive back inside to warm up and settle in once again. He glanced at his watch expecting to see a much later hour: 9:30 p.m. seemed to laugh back at him. He knew he was in for a long night and potentially an even longer journey.

The son of a businessman and the grandson of a lawyer, Yonason graduated from the University of California with an English degree and with intentions of making a real difference in the world. As a self-described introvert, Yonason saw this stage of his life as an opportunity to change. He wanted to put himself in positions that would make him extremely uncomfortable and expand his comfort zone. After graduating college, Yonason quickly understood that his English degree was not very marketable. He also realized that he no longer wanted to follow in his father's or grandfather's footsteps. And so, he did what any young twenty-something would do in the early 1980s — he set out to find himself through a pursuit of wanderlust.

What followed would be decades of domestic and international travel, curating a resume which reads more like an adventure novel than a professional summary of accomplishments. As Yonason reminisces, he would be the first to tell you that, when he was in the midst of making these decisions, they looked much different than they do now in hindsight. As he muses over his adventures, he can see definite points of unexpected transitions, and never would have dreamed that he would be where he is today when he set out to see the world some forty years ago.

Ironically, after that first and horrible night, he almost called it quits. If he had, I may have never had the chance to interview him and the world would not know his adventures or benefit from his hard-earned wisdom. However, before leaving home, he had told just about every person he knew about his trip, and the thought of crawling back, hat in hand, weighed heavier on his conscience than one rough night's sleep. That metaphorical storm was much scarier to him than the one he survived on night number one.

With the oncoming winter soon upon him, and a desire to escape the recent memory of almost-failure, Yonason hitchhiked his way as far South as he could. He eventually took up residence in the Florida Keys. Now on island time, and not wanting to spend his time flipping burgers or working other menial, low paying jobs, he took to hanging around the docks to see if he could get a job on a shrimp boat. In his mind, this would be the most exciting way to both make a living and learn what he was made of.

After weeks of asking around, only to be told that no one knew of any jobs and if he just simply "asked around" he would find a job — initiating a vicious cycle, living up to the definition of insanity — Yonason caught his break. He ended up landing a job ferrying confiscated boats from Southern Florida to Northern Florida for the U.S. Coast Guard. Southern Florida can be a popular spot for smuggling contraband, and when the Coast Guard makes a bust the boat-in-question is impounded up North until the trial is over.

Yonason's job was to ride in the confiscated boat as it was ferried North. If the confiscated boat started to sink, his job was to cut the rope that connected it to the tug so that both boats didn't perish. One day he would be riding on a dilapidated motorboat, holding on for dear life; and the next, he would be laid back and suntanning on some dubious yacht. It was 1983 and he was making $45 a day. By prioritizing only the essentials and living in youth hostels, Yonason was able to live on just $10 a day — not a bad gig.

After a few months, he had collected quite a number of adventures. He met fellow travelers from all over the world and had absolutely achieved his initial goal of getting outside of his comfort zone. One day, Yonason called home to let his parents know he would be making his way back. He accomplished his goal and it was time to re-enter society. His mother said that she had heard about a graduate school program at the University of London and asked him if he wanted to go. Yonason really did not want to extend his travels. At this point he was craving a taste of the "normal" life he had initially been escaping. But his mother persisted and even signed him up for classes against his will, and without his knowledge. Begrudgingly, Yonason arrived in London and enrolled in the program. It didn't take long for his sense of adventure to kick back into overdrive and he spent another six months traveling all over Europe — arguably spending more time on trains than in the classroom.

It was here that his years of traveling across the United States, and now Europe, began to take its toll. One day, Yonason found himself on a street corner in Vienna simply unable to decide which way to turn next. He had reached total decision fatigue. Deep down, Yonason knew that it was time for him to trade travel for a true vacation.

Throughout his adventures and time spent interacting with others from all around the world, he had heard about Kibbutz in Israel. There you could work the land and stay for free, reinvigorating your soul through honest labor. He decided this sort of a reprieve from everyday decision making was just what he needed and made his way to Tel Aviv. However, what Yonason failed to realize at the time was that the United States Dollar was at an all-time high. As such, Europe was flooded with Americans; many of whom had the same notion of chasing the minimalist Kibbutz lifestyle. So, when he arrived at the placement office in Tel Aviv, instead of finding his reprieve, Yonason found hordes of people camping out in sleeping bags, waiting for openings. A sign read that there were no more openings and to come back next year. Not what he was hoping for.

Just as he had learned of the solace offered by a Kibbutz in his travels, Yonason had also heard about Yeshivas. A Yeshiva is a type of rabbinic seminary for Jews without much knowledge of their ancestral and religious backgrounds. They offer a chance for those interested in a sort of catch-up-course on their religious education. With no room on the farms, Yonason enrolled in a Yeshiva as his next best option for rest from his travels.

He was surprised at what he found there. Instead a mental retreat, Yonason fell in love with the intellectual discipline of it all; with the way it challenged his mind. The more he stayed, learned, and argued with the Rabbis, the more he fell in love.

After extending his European excursion, Yonason fell in love with more than his Jewish faith. He not only became a Rabbi himself, but also met his wife, got married, started a family, and ended up living in Israel for nine years before finally making his way back to the United States.

Now, he travels the country teaching ethics to both students and businesses and sharing his message whenever possible on podcasts like mine. Yonason was actually one of the first people to reach out to me and request to be on the show, instead of me having to seek out his interest. I had no idea what I was in for when I quickly agreed to broadcast his story. Through the course of our conversation, it became clear that Yonason developed the ability to adapt the theological teachings he grew to love in Israel into secular programming. This allows his message to have mass appeal, regardless of someone's religious background. Expanding on this idea, his popular TEDx talk aims to have everyone question the foundation of their belief system. Yonason muses that if we take the time to actually question our values and what we believe, as well as how we came to believe it, that we might not be able to defend those beliefs as well as we'd like. If anyone is qualified to ask those types of questions, certainly the man with an adventure novel for a resume fits the bill.

TAKEAWAYS

As a newly minted college graduate, Yonason set out on a journey that began with a narrow focus and evolved to be larger than life. Literally, larger than any life he ever imagined for himself. His initial goal of shedding his identity as an introvert, evolved into his present-day status as an international speaker and sought-after expert on ethics.

Part of Passive Unseen Work is exposing yourself to different people and different ideas. On their own, these unique circumstances seem to be just that — unique. But stitched together over time, patterns emerge, and experiences build upon one another to create impact. Lasting impact. It is easy to think about each of our singular endeavors as just that: singular. However, every experience we take in alters us slightly and enriches the foundation for the next experience. This cycle continues for the entirety of our lives.

When I spoke with Yonason and initially captured the story

you just read, I was struck by the power of his decision to stick it out after his tent collapsed on night one of his journey. While most people would have seen that as a bad omen and a sign that they were not meant to keep going, he took it on the chin, put his head down and got the work done. In many ways, that's a fitting description of how he approaches other areas in his life.

When I shared this thought with him, he took my observation one step further, sharing with me something he learned from his days on the water ferrying confiscated boats: a sailboat can actually go *faster* by cutting *into* the wind than with the wind at its back.

If we apply this idea to our own lives, when we lower our shoulders and force ourselves into the wind, things eventually feel easier and we start to move faster, but only because we have gotten stronger, not because the wind let up. By putting ourselves in compromising positions, we become more capable for the next storm that heads our way. In a way, Passive Unseen Work is one unexpected storm after another. It's how we choose to show up and stand up to that headwind that decides whether we grow stronger or if we're blown over.

From a collapsing pup tent, to a near mental break in Vienna, Yonason may have been slightly blown off course, but he never gave into those winds. In the end, he learned that he was never blown off course at all. Instead, the universe simply adjusted course for him and brought him to the path he explores today. Where he was meant to be.

He did not set out to build a personal brand, deliver keynotes speeches or become a Rabbi. However, his propensity to take the road less traveled has allowed him to consume the wide variety of experiences, cultures, and personalities this world has to offer. The end result, after years of compounded Unseen Work, has brought us a respected thought leader and religious scholar.

CHAPTER 12:
CHOOSING JOY

A sea of white pages, black lettering and tongue-twisting legalese covered every knot of wood on the dining room table. As the mother of two dialed the number for her point of contact at the Internal Revenue Service, she held her breath and prayed to hear a friendly voice on the other end. While everyone she dealt with at the IRS was certainly helpful, they were also sure to remind her, whenever possible, that most people simply hired a lawyer to navigate the process she was so keen to stumble through without any formal legal education. But, as a single mother working three jobs and launching a non-profit, excess funds for legal counsel were simply not an option.

After three years of hustle and hard work, her paperwork was approved, funding came through, and our dining room district attorney was able to quit those three jobs and focus on the two she was most passionate about — her children and delivering free meals to homebound cancer patients. Allow me to introduce Jennifer Caraway, founder of The Joy Bus and The Joy Bus Diner.

According to Jennifer's website, thejoybusdiner.com:

"The Joy Bus is a Not for Profit organization whose sole purpose is to relieve the daily struggles of homebound cancer patients with a fresh

Chef Inspired meal and a friendly face. Our vision is to elevate the livelihood of our patrons with the joy of culinary sustenance. Founded in 2011 and named in honor of our dear friend Joy who struggled with the painstaking side-effects of cancer, ultimately losing her life to this horrific disease. Joy suffered from cancer in the 4 "L" s (in Joy's words) "Lungs, Liver, Lymphoid and Loveries". Her drive and determination are inspirational to all those who fight her same battle and if a hot meal and a little compassion can brighten her day then it's the least we can all do as humans and as a part of a community. Millions of cancer patients are left to fend for themselves during this turning point in their lives. The Joy Bus will relieve the burden put on families during this time by providing healthy meals specified to meet our patron's needs. The Joy Bus delivers not only quality meals to your doorstep but compassion and a smiling face."

Jennifer is a self-described latchkey kid of the 1970s, who spent much of her after school time alone at home and with little to no adult supervision. She would often be on her own for dinner and became skilled at creating full meals with what little she had available to her in her home. To this day, she can do some amazing things with a pack of Ramen. While her cooking skills were born out of necessity, they quickly blossomed into a passion and a way to express herself creatively. Food became Jennifer's favorite form of art.

As soon as she was old enough to get a job, she began washing dishes at a Mexican restaurant in a nearby shopping mall. It may not have been a Michelin star establishment, but to Jennifer it might as well have been. She couldn't get enough of the kitchen's intensity and worked her way up from dishes to a line cook, and eventually to a management position. In the process of working her way up the ladder, she knew deep down that one day, she would have a place of her own.

When the time came for Jennifer to attend college, she opted for the Hotel and Management program at Northern Arizona University. However, after three years of school Jennifer found herself yearning to return to the fast-paced lifestyle of a kitchen line. Having already worked her way through the ladder of the industry she was studying to work within, she came to the realization that her own life experience was way more valuable than paying someone to tell her what direction to take or the path she should take to get to where she had already been. College exists to serve some people, but Jennifer discovered she was not one of those people. At her core she's wired to jump in and figure it out for herself — with her hands on a knife and the heat from a stove top tanning her skin. She traded the classroom for some cast iron, dropped out of school, and moved to Portland to open her own restaurant.

She's never looked back.

If that was the end of Jennifer's story, it would still be remarkable. It takes guts to realize a passion, take action towards it at a young age, begin a pursuit of conventional definitions of success, and then ultimately go against the grain by dropping out of school. Further, the drive required to start a business, especially one as complex as a restaurant, cannot be understated. However, this only marks the beginning of Jennifer's journey.

After that first restaurant in Oregon, Jennifer pursued additional culinary endeavors and eventually found herself back in Arizona around 2009. It was then that her good friend Joy was diagnosed with ovarian cancer. Not knowing the best way to be there for her friend during such a rough time, Jennifer turned to what she knew best. Food. She started making Joy small treats and hand-delivering them to her while she recovered at home from treatments. Her homemade food, paired with empathy and conversation, went a long way to comfort Joy.

Unfortunately, Joy passed away. However, Jennifer's conviction did not pass. She sought out organizations that specialized in providing the service she had informally delivered to Joy and was surprised to find nothing.

One night, after struggling to fall asleep, Jennifer rolled out of bed and switched on the television. After mindlessly zapping from channel to channel, she found herself immersed in the movie *Mr. Holland's Opus* – a dramatic film detailing the effect one music teacher had on hundreds of his students. So, at 2:30 a.m. Jennifer found herself pondering the meaning of life and questions like:

What impact am I making on the community?

What kind of role model am I being for my children?

Why aren't I doing anything to help anyone other than myself or my kids?

As humans shouldn't we be doing something to help society as a whole?

At that moment, Jennifer vowed to commit herself to a cause greater than just one person. And, in 2011, "The Joy Bus" was born.

Jennifer began by cooking meals in her home kitchen and then personally delivering them to members of the community. When she reached fifteen home visits each week, the workload was too much for her residential kitchen to handle. Knowing that she would need to lease a commercial kitchen space, she convinced her non-profit's board of directors that, since they'd have to lease a kitchen regardless, they might as well open it to the public as a restaurant. That way, they could sell food and use the proceeds to further fund the mission of the nonprofit. *It worked like a charm.*

Quickly, Jennifer went from fifteen visits a week, to fifty! Both the surrounding restaurant communities and local residents have been ultra-supportive of the mission to provide beautiful and organic, free meals to at home cancer patients. Local farmers donate left-over produce, fellow chefs donate their time or run specials at their own restaurants to support fundraising, and local community members volunteer to make deliveries and deliver both food and companionship to the patients.

When things get hard — and between managing a restaurant, a

non-profit, and the family household, they do — Jennifer draws on stories of how The Joy Bus continues to impact the community for strength. When she hears how receiving meals and companionship eases the burden of cancer treatments and how giving of their time is transformative for volunteers, it reminds her of that 2:30 a.m. feeling that set the whole journey in motion. This mindset is truly indicative of Jennifer. She much prefers to be in the kitchen: behind the scenes and out of the spotlight.

However, after years of work and countless hours in the kitchen, the spotlight came calling.

Jennifer wasn't at the diner when the call came in, so the front of house manager took the message and delivered it some hours later. When Jennifer heard that producers from Food Network's *Chopped* called and were interested in speaking with her, she almost didn't return the call. She was convinced it was a prank. Even if it wasn't a prank, she had made her mind up that she was just too busy running her businesses to pursue her fifteen minutes of fame.

However, when Jennifer shared the story of the so-called prank with her children over family dinner, her daughter insisted that she return the call. *Chopped* was her daughter's favorite show, and she pointed out how it could be a perfect exposure opportunity for The Joy Bus. So, reluctantly, Jennifer returned the call.

It was, in fact, real. No joke. Jennifer met with the producers and agreed to participate in the show as long as the focus was either on charities, fellow diner-cooks, or both. She did not want to go up against "real" chefs, as she did not feel she fell into that class of culinary expertise.

Weeks later, she received an email with a date, time, and location for filming. Her prodding to find out if her request regarding a charitable or diner-related tie-in, went unanswered. But, she flew to New York anyway.

In addition to the basic instructions explaining where and when to show up, the email also stressed the importance of Jennifer bringing her own knives. As a chef's knives are akin to a homebuilder's tool belt or a painter's brush collection, the show would not be providing these instruments of the craft.

A quick Google search on professional chef knife sets will tell you that most sets contain eight, distinctly different knives; each serving its own purpose. Jennifer, as a self-proclaimed cook and not a chef, had one knife. One.

Armed for culinary battle with her one, trusted blade, Jennifer stepped onto the television set at five-thirty in the morning. As she made her way past the other contestants and to her station, it became clear that this was not going to be an episode starring diner chefs or well-intentioned non-profit owners. A mix of small talk and the vast array of glistening stainless-steel told Jennifer that she would be competing against the real deal. While she could have lost her cool and let this realization get to her, she held her composure.

In fact, without even realizing it, Jennifer had been training her whole life for this show. *Chopped* puts its contestants through a gauntlet of challenges; forcing them to create creative dishes from hodgepodge offerings of ingredients. Jennifer had done this her whole life. As a child, her pantry was one giant *Chopped* basket — remember her affinity for Ramen noodle creations? At the helm of The Joy Bus Diner, she was at the mercy of donations from local farmers to create meals for her customers. Forcing her to think on her feet every day to deliver on her promise to those in need.

Jennifer walked onto that television set with just one knife. She walked out a *Chopped* Champion.

TAKEAWAYS

If you had asked Jennifer the day she decided to start washing dishes at a Mexican restaurant if she would end up owning several of her own restaurants, steering a non-profit, or winning a reality TV cooking competition, she might have looked at you cross-eyed, but I don't know if she would have called you crazy.

Jennifer told me that she wakes up every day and feels like she is the luckiest person in the world. In fact, throughout our conversations, the word "luck" came up quite a bit.

In my opinion, luck is something that is curated. From Jennifer's story, we can see specific moments when decisions were made, and chances were taken. Often, the proverbial road-less-traveled was selected. When things got hard, Jennifer didn't run away. When the kitchen got hot, she didn't get out. She rolled up her sleeves and got to work. To me, that's not luck. That's *grit*.

Jennifer didn't start her career with the goal of being on television. In fact, her ambitions were toward the opposite end of the spectrum. Ironically for her, all of that time spent out of the spotlight is exactly what prepared her for her moment on center stage. By digging in and focusing on her love for cooking and focusing on how she could best serve others, she developed a world-class ability to improvise and perform under pressure. The exact skill set needed to win a televised cooking competition like *Chopped*, where the ability to create culinary magic from a basket of seemingly impossible ingredients, in insanely short timelines is rewarded with thousands of dollars in prize money.

This is Passive Unseen Work at its finest. Chances are the chefs she competed against wanted to be in front of that camera from the moment they first saw a show on The Food Network. This vanity probably led them to develop a persona that would be perfect on camera and appeal to the over-the-top antics which frequent the reality television genre. To be fair, they were also excellent at their craft. However, by focusing on themselves and not on something deeper and broader than a singular person, they ended up playing second fiddle to a diner cook with just one knife.

Passive Unseen Work shows us that it's not about being the flashiest, the best educated or the most well-known. It's about being the most prepared. There is a reason why people say it's the quiet ones you should watch out for. The people who aren't busy talking are busy listening and are busy learning. They are getting ready for their opponents to take a much-needed breath or to lose either focus or interest. When they make their move, most people never see it coming.

It's also worth noting the Generational Unseen Work at play

with Jennifer. On top of all she has accomplished through her passions in cooking and philanthropy, she also successfully raised two adults all on her own. As a single mother and entrepreneur, she's brought her children along to everything. They have had front row seats for every new restaurant she's opened, for the early days of The Joy Bus and for the big, televised *Chopped* victory. Her children have grown up watching their mother find balance in life and work, while also giving back to her community and to those in need. They've seen her strive towards personal and professional mastery and never let the fact that she only had one knife hold her back.

Earlier in this book, I presented the idea that children are mirrors. Before they even learn a spoken language, they learn the language of their parent's actions and begin speaking it fluently. Jennifer may count herself lucky, but truly the luck belongs to her children. The actions they have witnessed and will undoubtedly internalize and reflect in their own pursuits, are truly second to none. Jennifer's drive and determination, both seen and unseen, from the foundation upon which her children will begin their own journeys.

CHAPTER 13:
THE RENAISSANCE WOMAN

Erin Surrock spent the earliest days of her youth in the great Prairie State of Illinois. However, her father's profession as a project-based engineer meant that people in the company did not often stay in one place for long. As one project ended, another would begin and not necessarily in the same town, state, or even country. Erin joked with me, saying that in her father's company people did not ask you where you were from. Instead, they asked you where your family lived. Or, more bluntly, where you left your kids.

However, understanding the importance of stability in a child's life, when Erin's family moved to Maryland during her middle school years, her father decided to bounce between various jobs at his company's Maryland locations to ensure that she would be able to stay in the same place through high school graduation.

As a child, Erin's parents were the kind that didn't believe in failure. If she didn't succeed at something it simply meant she did not try hard enough. Now, at first pass, this may seem over the top. To some, perhaps even cruel. However, looking back, Erin appreciates this about her parents. To be sure, she was constantly frustrated with them in those moments. What angsty teenager wouldn't be? Today, as a well-adjusted adult in her thirties, she knows that those teachable moments of her youth actually prepared her to be better at life than most people.

Erin's parents imparted such lessons through several small, yet influential parenting practices. As a teenager if Erin was having an issue with her phone, her father would insist that she call the phone company and talk to the customer service representative. He did not do it for her. Instead of simply buying her a puppy when she was younger, Erin was encouraged to develop a PowerPoint presentation on all the reasons why receiving one was a good idea. Before popularization of the internet, when Erin's mother wanted to call a business to see if they carried a particular product, Erin was instructed to comb through the phone book, find the correct number, and then complete the cold call on behalf of her mother. Can't you just imagine the pubescent eye rolls during each of those lessons?

Erin was both a diligent student and a multi-sport athlete during her high school career. However, due to an unfortunate knee injury and its associated complications, the athletic portion of her career was cut short. With athletics off the table, Erin focused solely on academics; fulfilling her graduation requirements ahead of schedule and allowing her to apply for early graduation. At her parents' chagrin, Erin graduated high school a year early, at seventeen years old, and enrolled as a college freshman before her eighteenth birthday. Shortly after she began her collegiate studies, her father accepted a new project assignment in England — setting in motion life events that would push Erin out of her comfort zone and allow her to fully flourish.

Back when I interviewed Sarah Nuse, founder of Tippi Toes Dance Company, she shared this idea with me that, as a parent, the goal is not to have perfect kids. The goal is to raise self-sufficient adults. In hindsight, it would seem Erin's parents also subscribed to this idea. It was as if they knew that one day the assignment in England would come, because by the time it did, they had raised Erin to be completely self-sufficient. All before her eighteenth birthday. It's a good thing, too. Erin's parents did not move back to the United States until 2019, meaning that she spent over a decade in this country without them.

The Surrock family value of continuing to persevere, instilled in her the value of persistence and the notion that it is always possible for her to figure things out on her own. For Erin, things are always surmountable. This mindset has laid the foundation for the Unseen Work we are about to unpack.

Buckle up — it's quite the pedigree.

When Erin graduated from college in 2010, with a degree in graphic design, it was not an ideal time in the job market to be a newly minted college graduate. After returning from volunteer work in Mississippi, in response to the Deep-Water Horizon Oil Spill, Erin started the arduous task of finding a job in her field of study. Every entry level job she applied to seemed to demand at least six years of experience. While Erin had held an on-campus design position throughout college, as well as an internship at American Online (AOL), she still struggled with the paradox of finding entry level work in order to qualify for more entry level work.

After submitting so many job applications that her email service began marking "thank you for your application" emails as junk mail, the seed of an idea came to Erin in a moment of frustration. After spending months applying to jobs and not even receiving rejections, just deafening silence, she told her friend she might as well stand on the street corner with a cardboard sign that says, "will work for money." As it turns out, that was not such a bad idea.

Armed with her skills as a graphic designer and tech savvy twenty-something, Erin did, in fact, make that cardboard sign. But, instead of standing on an actual street corner, she created a virtual one. She built a website that consisted of a simple landing page, showcasing Erin holding her cardboard sign as well as the following paragraph:

"What sets me apart from the millions of others? Why should you hire me over anyone else? To try and convince you the old-fashioned

way, you can read my resume, contact me, or find out more about me.

However, I like to do things a bit differently. You can also read this haiku, check out these samples of work, consider this list of reasons, or connect with me on various social networking sites."

On the site, Erin's text references to her resume and portfolio were also hyperlinks to additional webpages which included those pieces of information. This approach offered employers insight into her wit and personality, in addition to quantitative facts and reasons to hire her. HireSurrock.com was a hit. It still is by the way — go ahead and check it out!

Armed with her "try hard enough" mindset and knowledge that anything is surmountable, her stunt worked. After just a few weeks of altering her application strategy to focus attention to her new website, Erin landed a job at a popular craft brewery in Baltimore. In her interview, they even quipped that she was "the one with the funny website."

After working at the brewery for two years designing artwork for their website, packaging, and apparel, Erin started to feel as if she was plateauing. Seemingly born with a fear of being the smartest person in the room, she began to realize herself advancing toward that dreaded title and she felt compelled to make a change. This feeling wasn't born out of arrogance, but a search for something more. The desire to continuously stretch and expand her comfort zone.

So, what did she do? Well, naturally, she started her own business.

Erin and a friend began their own screen-printing company. They had no idea what they were doing, but somehow figured it out. By now, this should be of no surprise to you. The company was growing, but still not bringing in enough for her to live on, so she took up some odd jobs.

Fun fact: turns out you do not need any formal certifications to be an orthodontist's assistant. So, at that point in her history, you could find Erin cranking out t-shirts at night and helping doctors apply braces to the mouths of young children during the day.

Erin's creativity did not just stop at graphic design or digital media — or even tricks for bedside manner with brace-faced teenagers. She grew up playing music, joining her first rock band in high school, and is fluent in the love language of bass guitar. One day while cruising Craigslist, she responded to an ad by a local band looking for her particular set of skills. After a few trial jam sessions, she hit it off with the group and joined as their bass guitarist.

They were good. Really good.

Good enough to get a spec deal from a record label. This means that the label paid to have them record an album and then helped promote the sale of that record and ticket sales for live shows. Since the record label had paid for the album to be recorded, they had a vested interest in the band's performance and allocated significant resources towards their promotion.

Erin quit her job putting braces on teeth and temporarily shuttered the t-shirt business. Thus, began her rock star chapter, beginning with a trip to Los Angeles to record an album. While out there, the band was able to play the Viper Room — a prestigious venue known by any serious music fan. After that, the band ventured across the pond for a European tour. They started in Italy and then drove through to Scotland where they played several sold-out shows.

Sadly, as most music journey's end (typically before they truly ever get started), there was a falling out among members of the band and the group parted ways. Erin dusted off her college degree and got back to work, focusing on reigniting her design career. Along the way, Erin continued to collect relationships with new people and grow a very diverse network of contacts. It was one of these contacts that posted about a freelance job on Facebook and encouraged Erin to apply. With a bit more on her resume than her first crack at the job market, she landed the gig easily. With NASA.

The freelance position was designing the transition binder which would be handed off to the landing team of the incoming presidential administration. Erin and her team of several other designers were tasked with organizing all of the information in a way that was concise, informative, and easily digestible.

At the time, most transition binders were literal binders. Think middle school trapper keepers bulging with printed documents. Erin and her team designed a way to have all the information electronically optimized and preloaded into iPads. Their goal was to have administration staffers gossiping about how cool it was over beers after work in D.C. The contract paid handsomely, and by the hour. Because Erin was the only designer on the team, she would work from 11:00 a.m. to 7:00 a.m. creating content, then submit her work for revisions. Grab a few hours of sleep. Then wake up and repeat the cycle. This went on for several weeks until the work was done. The inauguration waits for no man or woman. While the job was grueling, she learned a lot and was mentored by some powerful and inspirational women who managed to hold their own in a space dominated by male figureheads. An experience which Erin counts as life changing.

As a way to celebrate the end of the project, Erin mapped out a cross country road trip. Over the years, several of those relationships she had curated were with people who had moved elsewhere across the United States. Her goal was to visit all the people who told her to come visit. You know, those interactions, you promise that you will visit — but for one reason or another, the trip never happens.

She had saved up enough money from eating, sleeping, and working NASA that she thought she would be able to swing it. Plus, after weeks of enslavement to her computer screen, some windshield time with the open road felt like a much-needed reprieve. Erin never expected that the project would evolve into anything past the inauguration. While she was diligent about applying to jobs throughout the entirety of the project, in an attempt to have something else lined up upon its completion, she always expected an inevitable bout of unemployment, and was diligent about saving her money throughout the experience as a way to fund her future road trip plans.

When she was getting set to leave, one of those female mentors she had connected with reached out to her, complimented her on her work and, surprisingly, offered her a full-time job with the agency. The best part? It was 100% remote. Meaning that Erin was still able to embark on her road trip. As a bonus, since she was no longer traveling while unemployed, she was able to see and do way more than she originally thought would be possible.

Perhaps it was her newly found taste of the open road, or maybe that inner voice telling her she must never get too comfortable, but after two years at NASA, she began to feel that plateau-itch once more and decided to leave the agency.

Erin now works for a startup — meaning she has the freedom to continue fueling her love of travel. The company, an industrial control systems cyber security startup (try saying that three times fast) boasts the following tagline: *safeguarding civilization.* Meaning their goal is to protect the industrial technologies we all rely on from becoming compromised. A mission that perfectly aligns with Erin's diverse, and global, life experiences.

Fully leaning into her newfound identity as a digital nomad, Erin bought a 1986 Chevy G20 camper van, gutted it, and then set out on building it into a functioning tiny home — all by watching videos on YouTube. Again, nothing is insurmountable. It took her over a year, but after a few setbacks, she finished her van restoration near the end of 2019.

Now, she awakes each morning with her bulldog, Lucy, in whichever city, campsite, or Planet Fitness parking lot she chooses. Armed with the confidence that comes from playing sold out shows from Los Angeles to Scotland, starting her own business, working for NASA, and living on her own from age seventeen on, Erin is poised for even greater adventures in the years to come.

TAKEAWAYS

When I interviewed Erin for the podcast, I knew about one tenth of what I just recapped here. She was dating a friend of mine at the time, and I had a few people tell me she was interesting and had a story worth sharing. After I heard a version of this synopsis for the fifth time, I asked her to be a guest on the show. My buddies completely undersold her. In over 100 episodes, Erin has, by far, the most unique collection of life experiences I have encountered.

You may even be wondering why I've categorized her exploits as Passive Unseen Work. The process of churning out a transition binder for NASA, recording an album and touring Europe, starting your own business, learning to build a tiny home on YouTube, and the dozens of other life experiences Erin shared that did not make it into this final edit, are all very active pursuits. But we're not talking about each one in a vacuum. We're talking about the entirety of Erin – all of her experiences and the combined effect they have on how she shows up in the world. That is, by definition, Passive Unseen Work. When a vast array of seemingly unrelated items converges to create an outcome which we could never set out to accomplish from the start.

Erin, herself, hadn't really stopped to think about it this way until I pointed it out to her. That's the beauty of this idea. Most people don't. To us, our own lives are just that — life. Who really stops to think about the macro-level impact of their micro-level actions on a consistent basis?

As I have mentioned before, my hallmark question of the podcast is for the interviewee to describe their life in three words. Erin's three were: unique, enjoyable, and serendipitous.

Serendipitous. At the time it did not register, but now I can see that this work is a true synonym for Passive Unseen Work. Erin explains that she chose serendipitous because, when she looks back on her life, she realizes that a lot of the things she has accomplished have been due to her being in the right place, at the right time, talking to the right people, asking the right questions, and doing the right things. In the moments they initially occur, these individual experiences could be seen as coincidental. However, when compounded, they become *serendipitous*. All of Erin's seemingly unrelated experiences helped her in growing an expansive and diverse overall network of personal and professional connections. These connections would then fuel the next experience, and so on — continuing in a never-ending cycle.

I encourage you all to go back and re-read the overview I have given of Erin's story now that you have the lens of Passive Unseen Work front and center in your mind. I'm willing to bet that you can draw some parallels between her life and your own.

I know I can. When I was growing up, if I brought home a grade of 98% on a school project, my parents would ask me what happened to the other two percent. I was made to order food from the deli, order pizza, sell Boy Scout popcorn door-to-door, etc. Like Erin, at the time, I very much hated every minute of what felt like torturous prodding from my parents. But, as an adult, I am now well equipped to be comfortable when I am uncomfortable, and to always strive to be better. Sure, when taken in hard polarities, this can be unhealthy. But it's up to me to find that balance, and I work at it every day.

I'll leave you with one more story about Erin. When she and her partner were trying to name their screen-printing company, they agonized over options. To the point where the people closest to them became increasingly annoyed by this inability to decide. One of her friends told her to just name the company JFPO:

"Just Fucking Pick One."

In our podcast together, Erin tells that story through fits of laughter, however, the lesson here should not get lost in an errant curse word. Nor should it be dismissed as a joke. It's really a profound statement. At the end of the day, as the famous quote goes: perfect is the enemy of good. If we give into analysis paralysis and fret over what may or may not happen, we'll never take action towards anything.

Erin's take on this is that if you find yourself rationalizing reasons not to do something in your head, that means you should absolutely do it. Because the time you've spent trying to convince yourself not to do something is time you could have been spending actually doing that thing.

And if you fail? So, what!? You can always go back to where you have been or to what you were doing before. But you can never go back to something that you never tried. Those who lean into an awareness of Passive Unseen Work truly embrace this notion of soaking up the lessons from every experience, no matter how small it may seem at the time. Eventually, these little experiences will add up to greatly affect who you are, what you are capable of, and how you see the world.

CHAPTER 14:
PASSIVE UNSEEN WORK SUMMARY

If Active Unseen Work is beginning with the end in mind, Passive Unseen Work is simply choosing to begin; without knowing where your actions may lead. Please, do not confuse passive Unseen Work with going with the flow. With the idea that you can let go and let God or whatever cliché you subscribe to as a way to feel content in mediocrity. Instead, an adoption of, or an appreciation for Passive Unseen Work, is akin to *choosing* your flow.

If you were to simply go with this new flow you have chosen, if you dove in headfirst and began to float along, blissfully ignorant to what is to come next, you will eventually drown. You will soon find yourself ill-prepared for the journey, out of supplies, exhausted from treading water, and with no boat or raft to rest upon. Undoubtedly, you'll look up to the heavens and string together elaborate curses, placing all the blame on external forces.

In reality, the art of Passive Unseen Work is more like building and captaining a boat, than it is an exercise in floating. You've chosen the flow you'd like to go along with and now you are preparing for that journey. You're researching the tides, calculating how much food and water will be necessary, learning to navigate by the stars — you get the idea. You're building up all of the supportive habits you will need for when that flow you have chosen inevitably diverts you from the path of least resistance and challenges you.

Because of all this preparation, when you finally cast off and join the chosen flow aboard your well-constructed vessel, you're ready. You're ready not only for the outcome you are hoping for but also for the outcome you will most likely receive – one you never could have anticipated before making your choice. The trick is realizing that you've been building your boat all along. When you can have a high enough self-awareness to notice Passive Unseen Work at play in your life, that's when the real magic starts to happen.

When Yonason set out on a cross country backpacking trip, he never would have forecasted living in Israel for almost a decade, becoming a Rabbi and embarking on a lifelong journey in the field of ethics. However, at each crossroads-moment on his journey the lessons he learned, people he met, and inner strength he built up during seemingly unrelated pursuits, helped to bolster is approach to new challenges.

As Jennifer toiled away for decades in other people's kitchens and then in her own commercial and philanthropic enterprises, she never dreamed of the spotlight. She didn't realize that by developing dozens of ways to prepare Ramen as a child, or that by building menus for cancer patients out of donated produce, she was training to become a *Chopped* Champion. But when she heard a producer yell "action" from beyond the frame and was taunted by glaring red numbers counting down from a digital clockface, she felt prepared and not panicked.

Erin had no idea that one day her ability to haggle with the phone company, present her case for a puppy via PowerPoint, or cold call businesses for her mother would prepare her for the world with a mindset that anything is surmountable. Now, that determined young girl is a perfectly adjusted thirty-something with NASA on her resume and a mobile command center, traveling the country and broadening her horizons one new city at a time.

Passive Unseen Work is choosing to reframe every experience

of our life. Instead of things happening to you, things are happening for you. Instead of feeling trapped in a room with your competitors, your competitors are trapped with you. Every experience, every encounter with a new person, and every perceived set back is only preparing you for something bigger and better than you could ever imagine. Focus on building your boat and strengthening your vessel and when the tide sweeps you away, you'll be ready for whatever the journey throws at you.

PASSIVE UNSEEN WORK PROMPTS:

1. Think back on your earliest childhood memories:
    a. What lessons from your parents do you still think about today?
    b. What is a moment that felt silly or useless at the time, but now you can see it as transformative?
2. What are some small experiences or personal interactions in your life that eventually gave way to a big moment?
3. When have there been times where the journey towards a goal has given you more enjoyment or fulfillment then reaching the goal itself?
4. How have certain experiences changed you as a person?
    a. And thus, changed the way you approach your next life experience?
    b. Or your next relationship?
5. If you could realize Passive Unseen Work at play while it was happening, instead of years after the fact, how could you harness it to your advantage?

The irony of Passive Unseen Work is that, if you don't recognize it as it's happening and if you take a passive approach to it, then it's not as effective. To be sure, put enough of it in and it will absolutely add up to something. However, that something may not be completely to your liking. By becoming aware of how seemingly unrelated experiences or relationships could combine to form a desired outcome, you become better equipped to steer yourself in the direction of your choice. By taking an *active* role in your Passive Unseen Work, you can better control the outcomes of every experience you have and new relationship you form. Now you may be asking yourself:

If I am steering my Passive Unseen Work, or taking an active role in it, wouldn't that just make it Active Unseen Work?

Can they be both at the same time?

Excellent questions! Let's dive into the answers.

NOTE: You don't have to sort through these prompts alone! Head over to www.mylesbiggs.com for information on the Unseen Work Mastermind. You can request more information, join the waiting list, and get access to a community of like-minded people who are putting in their Unseen Work – just like you.

PART 4:
BRIDGING THE G.A.P. OF UNSEEN WORK

CHAPTER 15:
LEVERAGING ALL THREE TYPES

The three different types of Unseen Work are not mutually exclusive. Active and Passive work do not exist in a vacuum. Generational Unseen Work is nothing more than the Active and Passive Unseen Work of those who have provided for our future opportunities. Active Work is a way of realizing the occurrence of Passive Work in your life and taking action upon it. Passive Work is really just a collection of unrelated Active Work pursuits.

You might need to reread that a few times before it really sinks in. For me, it's helpful to think of these ideas as mathematical equations:

Generational Unseen Work = Ancestral Active Unseen Work + Ancestral Passive Unseen Work

Active Unseen Work = Passive Unseen Work + Active Unseen Work

Passive Unseen Work = Active Unseen Work + Active Unseen Work

After you are comfortable with this idea of how each type can be intertwined, consider the following:

Active Unseen Work in one arena can also be Passive Unseen Work for a future moment in your life you have not thought of yet. However, once you realize this, it ceases to be *passive* as you now *actively* put it to work towards your defined goal or goals. Likewise, generational work continues to evolve as we learn more about our ancestors and as we continue to observe the way they show up in the world. In this way, the three types of Unseen Work are not passive at all, in and of themselves, but really their own living forms of energy – helping to steer every area of our lives.

Since Unseen Work is not linear, sometimes we will be both active and passive at the same time, while drawing upon generational forces to fuel each type of Unseen Work. The reason I chose the particular arrow you find on this book's cover and on the title page for each new section, is because it personifies this idea. Your life experiences are rarely arranged in a neat and orderly line, and neither is your accumulation of Unseen Work. Sometimes you must go backwards to go forwards or be upside down before you can be right side up. But, as long as you're moving forward, (eventually) you will reach the end you have in mind and (likely) even surpass it.

I know — this is a head scratcher. The following examples will further drive home this idea.

CHAPTER 16:
DO IT SCARED

Contractors marched in and out of the home: seamlessly moving about their various trades and giving the appearance of elaborate communication without uttering a single word. This deliberate choreography of construction would go on for months, with coordination akin to a troop of ants or hive of bees — each soldier dutifully carrying out his task as part of a grander design.

On this project, the man behind the design could be seen pacing back and forth and moving erratically when compared to his disciplined workforce. While everyone else seemed to communicate non-verbally, he could be seen muttering incoherently to himself and occasionally waving a smartphone in the air. For onlookers, it was impossible to know if he was insane or just searching for a stronger cell signal. His erratic behavior would continue for hours, until the final contractor exited the jobsite. Only then, after hours of mumbling and an intense mental dialogue, did the pacing stop. The man's feet found their roots and planted themselves confidently in the kitchen. His smartphone was extended in front of his face – revealing that the signal he had been searching for was really the perfect camera angle – and he began recording his first-ever live video feed.

This scene took place nearly five years ago. Since his first video, Dave Cooper has filmed hundreds of others just like it — taking viewers behind the scenes of his elaborate construction projects. What started as a forced exercise, thrust upon him from the social media manager he had hired to help promote his business, has now blossomed into a full-time endeavor. He has gone from shooting selfie-style, live social media videos, to purchasing professional cameras and microphones and getting paid to travel all over the country to attend and document events within the housing industry.

So, how does someone overseeing home building projects become an online influencer? While you may be envisioning Dave as a former digital marketing major in college or a once- hobbyist photographer reigniting an old passion, you would be several degrees off the mark.

In the late 1980s, Dave enlisted in the United States Army. With an inherently inquisitive mind, he's always been able to approach complex subjects with grace and, therefore, performed well throughout his training. When he completed his Army training in 1990, he entered active duty as a newly minted combat medic. Just in time for the United States to launch Operation Desert Storm.

Throughout multiple deployments overseas, he would spend a total of two full years in the Middle East. In his capacity as a combat medic, he was often serving where intense action was taking place. As the world was literally exploding all around him, he learned how to focus his attention on what he had to make happen, not what could possibly happen to him, or on any atrocities in his rear-view mirror. He harnessed this ability to compartmentalize to thrive as a medic and, after ten years of service, he reentered the civilian world in hopes of further pursuing a medical career.

Dave spent some time working odd jobs and assimilating back into society — a task that is no simple feat for anyone who has served in the military or seen combat. Eventually, he landed a job as a spinal implant representative for Johnson & Johnson in the New York City metropolitan area. After his training, orientation, and learning of his products, Dave went to work with neuro and orthopedic spine surgeons. It was his job to train them in the newest spinal implant products and how to use them with their patients. He would go so far as to buy cadavers and run hands-on workshops with physicians to show them how to properly use the equipment. When it came time for the real deal, Dave would be in the operating room with the surgical team. He would use a laser pointer to guide nurses to the next item a surgeon would need and even recommend which screw sizes to use based on a patient's size and level of spinal stability.

After honing his ability to focus on the present moment and accomplish the mission as an Army combat medic, Dave thrived in his new civilian capacity. He was excellent at his job and forged lasting relationships with the surgeons he worked with. However, the sales side of the human-life-saving-business never sat well with Dave. He would often find himself in an ethical battle over how many physicians he could properly assist while still meeting his aggressive corporate sales goals.

This ethical dilemma was further fueled for Dave on September 11, 2001. Dave was working near New York City when the first plane made contact with The World Trade Center. Ever the soldier, Dave lived up to his oath to support and defend the Constitution of the United States against all enemies. While others were leaving the city, he found his way to where rescue boats were unloading wounded survivors. Dave immediately filled in the first responders of his military background and accepted their invitation to begin work. It wasn't long before Dave found himself on one of those rescue boats and headed directly into the city. He spent days working with coordinated ground forces, searching for survivors in the rubble, and triaging what injuries he could assist with.

After an experience like that, Dave knew he could not go back to juggling the priorities of a sales quota with lives hanging in the balance. He walked away from his job with Johnson & Johnson.

At the time, the real estate market was making a comeback and Dave had started to build spec homes on the side. The term "spec" in this instance refers to speculative — Dave would buy land and build a home on it with the intent to sell it immediately. Meaning that he was "speculating" about the location, the home, and the ability for it to sell quickly. This is common practice in the housing industry, especially in lucrative markets. Instead of speculating in stocks, folks with the proper skillsets like Dave, can turn their sweat equity into substantial capital gains.

While building his spec home, another developer purchased the building lot next to where Dave was building. Dave had been building his home the traditional way, by having all the materials delivered to his site and then constructing the home one piece of wood at a time. The person next to Dave, opted to employ off-site, modular construction. In this method, the home is constructed in pieces in a factory, then transported to the job site, and assembled using a crane. By using this method, Dave's neighbor was in and out of their job site, with the house sold and the family moved in, all before Dave had finished the plumbing on his job.

Dave was hooked. If he could orchestrate spinal surgeries and navigate the variables of combat medicine, he could certainly leverage third-party resources to scale and project manage construction sites. For a few decades now, he has been doing just that.

This brings us full circle to where we first met Dave, just a few pages ago. Now that he was not building everything himself anymore and had his coordinated crew of worker bees churning out homes for him, Dave had turned his attention to marketing and sales. He was now working on the business instead of simply in the business.

In trusting his social media manager, who recognized the trend towards video early on, Dave has been able to transform himself into a personal brand within the off-site housing industry. He has even begun expanding beyond his comfort zone of modular building and is growing a national following across the housing industry as a whole. Dave's videos grew to the point where customers began approaching him and selling him his own product: all because they watched his videos. Instead of arriving at his door uneducated, customers knew all about projects he had done for other customers and would simply tell him what they would like for him to do in their homes. Dave made the move from "selling" to simply fulfilling a need – something every business owner dreams of.

If Dave's story ended there it would be plenty noteworthy. But, in many ways he's just getting started.

When the COVID-19 Pandemic took hold in March 2020, lots of people began to retreat and took conservative stances in their businesses. The unknowns that came with stay-at-home orders, masks, social distancing, and reduced consumer spending sent many businesses into a downward spiral. But, for Dave, this was his moment. Pre-pandemic he was already in the process of forming his own media company, focused on documenting stories within the off-site construction industry. Now that a majority of the world was working from home and spending a significant amount of time on social media in search of connection and answers, Dave made a bold, public move: he committed to going live on LinkedIn, Facebook and YouTube six days a week for one year. Each day would have a different content focus, ranging from spotlighting housing industry products, interviewing experts on their fields, unpacking what it takes to build a personal brand, what's next for home building science, and more. While most established businesses were concerned with cashflow and payroll protection, Dave's scrappy startup was making a land grab. For months, much of the housing industry was sidelined; unable to go to jobsites.

So, where did they go?

Dave's social media profiles.

After maintaining his six-day-a-week live broadcasting habit for just six months, Dave left his full-time day job as a homebuilder and went all in on his own venture: Dave Cooper Live. Now he spends his days broadcasting live from his home studio and on-location at building sites and factories across the country. His shows have a global audience, and he has cemented his place as an influencer within the housing industry. All because he took consistent action and was able to compound all of his previous experiences into this new endeavor.

TAKEAWAYS

Before we fully unpack Dave Cooper's story, I'll give you some more context into how Dave and I began working together.

My friendship with Dave kicked off in Las Vegas, of all places. I'm not much of a gambler or a drinker, so ordinarily I would never take a trip to Sin City; however, a work conference and speaking opportunity brought me to Nevada and into Dave's path. I had known of Dave for a little over five years, but we had not spent much personal time together. He worked for a home builder that was a client of the modular home manufacturer I worked for at the time. So, up until this trip, all of our interactions had been surface-level and business oriented small talk.

Through the course of the conference, I learned that Dave also had a side passion project like mine. Where I had the podcast, Dave was building a personal brand around video. While at the conference, Dave was recording short videos to highlight various brands in attendance as a way to enhance his profile and portfolio, as well as network with industry stakeholders. In doing this, he was invited to a private event one night at the House of Blues and asked me if I wanted to tag along.

The event was for a group named Operation Finally Home, whose mission is to provide mortgage-free homes to service members and their families who have become wounded, ill, or injured as a result of their service in the defense of our country. That night they were holding a private concert for those who had supported them financially or otherwise that year, and they would also be announcing the next service member who would be receiving a home.

As a veteran, this was a cause near and dear to Dave's heart and there was no way he was going to miss a chance to show up and contribute. The event organizers agreed to let him bring his camera, so that Dave could interview attendees about their affiliation with the cause and then stitch together a promotional piece for the organization.

I had never been to the House of Blues before, and I was

expecting a typical, small corporate networking event. The idea that it was a free concert did not really resonate with me at the time. I simply assumed it would be a small local act — more of a gesture of "thank you" than a concert of any significance. However, shortly after arriving we learned that the main event would be award-winning, country music star, Craig Morgan.

At first, Dave and I had to awkwardly navigate cocktail conversations, approaching strangers about sticking a camera in their face. Initial recoils were met by Dave imposing small guilt trips since this was, of course, for charity after all. It took a few attempts, but eventually we were able to persuade our first volunteer. From there, that person recommended someone else we should talk to and provided an introduction. The next person did the same. Before we knew it, in the half hour before the concert began, Dave was able to interview six different people. It was a blast to watch him work the room!

As the house lights faded and the glow of colored stage lights took their place, followed by the low hum of amplifiers and the smooth, metallic flair of electric guitar strings, Dave and I faded into the rest of the crowd and reveled in the show. It's not often that you get to see a recording artist with several Billboard Top 10 and Number 1 songs, who normally plays arenas, serenading a group of a few hundred, just 25 feet from where you stand. It was truly a once in a lifetime experience.

As the music came to an end, we were notified that word had made it to the founder of the organization, and he wanted to make an on-camera appearance. So, we moved away from the loud crowd and located a semi-secluded portion of the event space to set up. I found myself holding an LED light stick above my head in one hand and working the camera for Dave in another as we rotated through the founder and several other dignitaries in attendance.

As we finished what we thought was going to be our last interview, I noticed several imposing men out of the corner of my eye. While I was trying to focus on keeping the light evenly distributed on Dave and his interviewee, I could not help but notice them moving towards us at a steadily increasing pace. As they got closer, it was evident that these men had never missed a meal in their lives. One might have even been half human and half Redwood tree. My initial thought was of the fact that we had no permit, no press badges, or any real claim as legitimate members of the media. Every cliché scene I had ever seen of schmucks being bounced from a nightclub replayed in my brain. Then, the Redwoods parted just feet in front of us and none other than Craig Morgan himself emerged. As a fellow veteran, Craig was also at the event to support his brothers and sisters in arms. When he heard there would be some promotional pieces made to advance the message, he found his way to Dave to give his two minutes on screen for the cause.

Twenty minutes later, it was around three o'clock in the morning and the event finally ended. Dave and I had both been awake for nearly twenty-four hours, but it felt like we had just mainlined Red Bull. We relived the evening over a drink, simply in awe of what our night evolved into. In that moment our relationship pivoted from vendor-client to creative comrades. We've worked on several creative and media driven side projects together in the years since. Ultimately, this memory I have with Dave is a perfect example of how different types of Unseen Work can converge.

Dave and I had both worked in the housing industry for years. Climbing the ladders in our respective companies until we both found ourselves at the industry's largest show in capacities other than mere attendees. It took some serious Active Unseen Work for each of us to get there.

Also, in addition to our day jobs, we had both spent years fueling our creative passions. I had built up my podcast, Dave had built up his vlogging and personal branding efforts, and we both learned to effectively navigate the vast array of audio and visual equipment required to create that content. Again, we had each put in our Active Unseen Work.

In Dave's case, he has also spent years serving in the United States Army as a combat medic, fulfilling the sense of duty he felt to God and country. When his time in the Army was up, he still upheld his oath of service and ran towards the fray on September 11, 2001 when most were headed in the opposite direction. Now, decades removed from his military service, Dave still seeks out opportunities to respect and honors his fellow veterans.

All of Dave's separate experiences led him to that moment at the House of Blues. Dave's previous service created his emotional pull towards supporting Operation Finally Home and his ability to relate to those in attendance. His years building up a personal brand through video meant that he had a unique skill to offer the organization in that moment. All of Dave's separate, Active Unseen Work pursuits, passively aligned in that moment — a moment he had no idea he's been preparing for.

This can happen to you too. Maybe it already has. I'm sure if you reflect back on moments of serendipity in your own life you can recognize some of the same elements discussed here.

It's moments like these that, I'll argue, prove that luck doesn't exist. Luck is simply putting yourself out there, over and over again, until you are eventually in the right place, and the right time, with the right skills, and surrounded by the right people. Then it's up to you whether or not you take advantage of it.

When it comes down to it, the only thing that makes Dave an expert on video, or a sought-after media influencer within the housing industry, is the fact that he took action. Not only did he take the first step, but he also kept walking, and he kept getting back up and continued to move forward even after falling.

Nothing worth pursuing in life is a one-and-done transaction. Becoming an expert takes time and practice. It takes an ability to live by one of Dave's favorite mantras: *Do it scared*. In fact, when you stop feeling a bit of nervousness or anxiousness as you're pushing towards your goals, that's when you should be worried. Without that it means you've gotten too comfortable, and it's time to start extending yourself further. That's the only way to keep growing and to keep leveling up.

It all comes down to intention. When we go out into the world each day, we can choose to have our intention dictated for us —

by locking into our favorite smartphone news and social feeds, growing numb to the world around us. Or we can consciously show up to what may seem to be trivial decision points, with the intention of pursuing greatness and helping others in everything we do. When that happens, and we do this repeatedly, stacking our efforts over and over — luck, serendipitous moments of synchronicity, or however else we choose to define often unexplainable moments, will begin to appear more frequently and in all areas of our lives.

It's not *lucky* that Dave's live broadcasts has secured him a place in the global housing conversations. It's not *lucky* that Dave is now getting flown across the country to cover housing industry events with his video camera. It's not *lucky* that he is getting invited to serve on boards of directors, or that companies are paying him to produce content. Whether it's been on the battlefield or in the boardroom, behind a surgical mask or behind a camera, Dave's intention to clear out the explosions life throws all around him, and put all of himself into the mission at hand, has allowed him to reinvent himself several times over. He's been able to transfer his Unseen Work with him each and every time and catapult his way to success.

CHAPTER 17:
BIG TOUGH GIRL

Each morning, Ashley Mitchell's day kicks off in the same way most parents' days begin. There are kids to wake up and wrangle, breakfast to make, lunches to prepare, and school buses to catch. Every parent I know will admit that, in some ways, we almost crave this twisted, three-ring circus. We all thrive on the pressure to provide for our little humans, and revel in the glory of a smile from our children, or a sweet 'thank you' muttered in a high-pitched, angelic voice. Once you have children and adjust to the idea that life will forever teeter on a fulcrum of fear, anxiety, and untold amounts of love, it's hard to imagine life without them. After the madness of early morning family rituals, the silence that creeps in throughout the day has most of us yearning for this madness to begin again. While we venture off into the lands of adulthood – careers, bills, and full-on adulting – our minds often wander to those little voices and our heart strings are played like a fiddle.

But, for Ashley, her fiddle is constantly lamenting; playing a song known only to a select few, and admitted to, by even fewer.

Much earlier in her life, Ashley found herself at the crossroads of a decision which would affect her life forever. She was in her mid-twenties and pregnant for the first time. However, she was not in a committed relationship, nor did she have the financial resources or emotional stability to parent her child. She had three options: parent the child, put the child up for an adoption, or have an abortion.

Ashley chose an open adoption.

An open adoption means that the adoptive family and the birth mother (in this case, Ashley) opt to stay in contact throughout the child's life. The adopted child knows from the very beginning that they have been adopted and have regular interaction with their birth mother, in addition to their adoptive parents. In comparison, a closed adoption would mean that the birth mother would have no contact with the adopted child, and it would be up to the adoptive parents to make the decision on whether or not the child knows of their adoption.

Ashley worked with a placement agency to identify potential parents and select the right family for her child. In this process, adoptive families put together a book which outlines who they are as a couple and a family, their values, their own reasons for wanting to adopt, and their vision for how the open adoption would function. From these books alone, Ashley had to make the decision on which family she would ask to adopt her child. Once she made that selection, these adoptive parents were invited along for the journey of her pregnancy and were even in the delivery room when her son was born. While in the hospital, Ashley was able to meet and hold her son for the first time before signing away her parental rights and sending him home with the adoptive family she had selected.

As you may imagine, for the first five years after she placed her son with his adoptive family, Ashley was heartbroken. Even though she knew she made the right choice for her child, it was still an excruciatingly difficult decision to make. Ask any woman and they will tell you about the physical and mental changes they undergo throughout pregnancy. It did not matter that Ashley didn't have her son with her, she was still a mother. Her pregnancy had changed her forever. Now she had to come to terms with the way her new life looked. While many people think adoption ends at the hospital, it is truly only the beginning of a long journey. Especially for Ashley.

As a childless mother, Ashley struggled to feel like she fit in anywhere and wrestled internally with how to vocalize her feelings. Her behavior grew increasingly self-destructive as she turned to drugs, sex, and alcohol to numb her feelings and escape the pain of reality. These activities led to a drunk driving accident and a small stint in jail, but her true rock bottom moment came after an ambulance ride to the emergency room turned into a five day stay at a mental health facility.

Sitting uncomfortably on her rock bottom, sheltered from the judgement of the outside world, Ashley began to take small steps toward recovery. A psychiatrist sat with her for those five days, stripping back the layers of her pain and refusing to accept her attempts to blow off vulnerability. It was not easy, but she emerged from the hospital ready to take her life back and to stop using her grief and trauma as an excuse to sit out on the rest of her existence. It took several years of work on herself, but Ashley did learn how to co-exist with that emptiness she felt as a now childless mother.

While on her downward spiral Ashley cut herself off from most of the world — including her son and his adoptive parents. She didn't quite know how to act around them. It had been pounded into her head that she would have no rights once she signed the adoption papers and it left her wondering if she could even ask to see her son. Not willing to go through the pain of rejection in addition to the pain she was already feeling, she simply fell off the face of the Earth.

After Ashley turned her life around, she got married and had more children, whom she and her husband are raising together. No longer a childless mother, she wanted to reconnect with her son and his adoptive parents. After reaching out to the family, they informed her, quite simply, that they had been waiting for her and wanted nothing more than for her to know their son. Things started off slow at first, with meetings in public spaces and the adoptive parents doing their due diligence to be sure she would be present and that she would respond to text and phone calls — cognizant of the fragility of a young boy's emotions. After proving herself to be reliable, these interactions between Ashley, the adoptive parents, and her son increased in frequency.

One day, Ashley was out shopping and felt the familiar sensation of her cell phone vibrating. She glanced down and joy began to immediately spread through every inch of her body. It was her son. He had texted her – on his own! He had been thinking about her and just wanted to check in and say hello. It was a full-circle moment for Ashley.

Today, this is how the relationship functions, it's all about what her son wants. He has a voice, he has his own needs and wants, and a power shift has taken place.

At the beginning of the adoption process, Ashley had the power. If she had changed her mind, she could have kept her child and the adoptive parents would have been forced to begin their process again. Once all the paperwork had been signed, the adoptive parents wielded the power. When Ashley reached out after years of silence, they could have easily told her she was not welcome. And now, the child is calling the shots and all three parents are doing their best to respect his wishes. From time to time, her son is even able to sleep over at Ashley's house, joining in that hustle and bustle of family mornings as described in the beginning of this section.

Families come in all sorts of shapes and sizes, colors, and creeds. But above all else — love makes a family.

TAKEAWAYS

Ashley Mitchell is one big, tough girl. Literally. That's her moniker on Instagram — @BigToughGirl.

Part of the work that Ashley did to claw herself up from rock bottom has involved speaking openly about her experiences as a birth mother. The adoption community is full of advocates and voices, however, the most prominent are often from the adoptive families. As Ashely began to add her side as a birth mother to the collective story, more and more people have stepped forward to do the same. She has had people from all walks of life reach out to her and explain that they are a "Big Tough Girl" who has gone through divorce, cancer, or who have had a child pass away. The core feelings of grief and trauma are universal, and Ashley is helping people all over the world avoid having to feel alone like she did.

One of Ashley's mantras is *"Own Your Shit."* She knows from experience how easy it can be to get stuck in a cycle of victimhood. Part of what allowed her to build her life back up was the decision she made to fight for herself. She knew she would not move forward if she did not take ownership of her own choices. For her, choosing to be a Big Tough Girl, means choosing to show up to her own life and to take control of it. Anger and avoidance are easy. Showing up and fighting is hard work.

She founded Lifetime Healing; a post-placement care network focused on providing training to adoption professionals. In this capacity, Ashley has authored the nation's first curriculum on post placement care. Today, she travels all over the country and trains adoption professionals, mental health professionals, and pregnancy centers on why women who relinquish the rights to their babies need free mental health support. From Ashley's perspective, the healthier a birth mother can be, the healthier the overall adoption will be. This is because if the adoptive parents are worrying about the birth mother, that stress eventually seeps into the entire family unit and has an effect on the adopted child. It does not serve the child (adopted or not) when adults are not able to handle their own baggage.

Ashley also offers a "Back to Basics" class as a way to educate hopeful adoptive couples. She works with them on how to handle themselves in the hospital around the birth mother, what to place in their books that will not be offensive, and how to best support the birth mothers after she relinquished her rights.

Part of Ashley's downward spiral was born out of her own lack of preparedness and how uneducated she was about the decision she was making. This has fueled her mission to make sure the same thing does not happen to others. Ultimately, she wants to remove the feeling of "why didn't someone tell me this?" for other people.

Adoption is not what *Lifetime* movies make it out to be. It often begins in complete brokenness. Grief can be isolating and makes people feel they are the only person on Earth going through the pain they are experiencing. But the more people who tell their stories, the less power grief has and the more confidence and cohesive the situation becomes. It's not about eliminating grief — it's about learning to live with it.

It can be easy to confuse anger with pain and hurt. Hurting people tend to be the ones who hurt people and social media can often fuel this fire. Private Facebook groups amongst members of the adoption community can be sources for "Mom Shaming" and can do more harm than good. Ashley's own experiences here also fuel her drive to create formal training programs and to bolster the actual professionals to better deal with these issues.

Her content is also great for those connected to people on the adoption journey. It can be hard to know what questions to ask (or not ask) and how to recognize birth mothers as the mothers they are. Adoption is truly a personification of the saying "it takes a village." The village is all of us — it's all of society.

Today, Ashley makes countless podcast appearances, films numerous educational pieces, gives keynote speeches at industry events, and much more. Each of these *seen* efforts is only possible because of the millions of moments of Unseen Work that led Ashley to the spotlight.

In the context of Unseen Work, the decision to speak out and share her story, on its own, was a piece of Active Unseen Work. After making that decision to educate the masses, using her own story as an example of the way things should not have to be, Ashley has taken purposeful strides towards that end every single day. However, Ashley would not have reached that moment if all of her previous experiences had not been passively building to that breaking point. Her ability to connect with her audience is born out of years of both self-destruction, and conversely, self-mastery. Ashley is able to use all of the trauma and grief of her past experiences as fuel for her life's passion and purpose. This focus on a cause greater than just one person can be a formidable motivator.

In an interesting way, Ashley's story and journey is also an example of Generational Unseen Work. All of her children, those she parents with her husband and her son whom she chose to put up for adoption, will grow up seeing their mother's passion, drive, and selflessness. They will know what it means to make mistakes, learn from them, and harness sacrifices into a power for good and to help others. They will see how love, not labels, truly makes a family; and their world will be broadened by their involvement in multiple family units. In time, as these children grow up, Ashley's experiences will have laid the groundwork for their own endeavors.

CHAPTER 18:
MR. ACTION

I have learned a great deal from a man named Dennis McGinley. Furthermore, without Dennis and the STRIVENT coaching community he has created, this book would just be a thought in my head and not a physical product existing in the world.

I met Dennis in an unorthodox way. In my pursuit to find guests for my podcast, I downloaded a networking app called Shapr — think Tinder for networking. You upload your professional profile and then swipe left on others if you don't see an opportunity to connect, or you swipe right if you'd like to see if collaboration is an option. So, while I was on this app looking for interesting people to interview, Dennis was on this app looking for people who would be a fit for his mastermind community of movers and shakers.

That first phone call with Dennis still makes me chuckle to myself. In our initial call, while I thought I was vetting him as a guest, he was vetting me as a possible coaching client. I knew that I was about to be sold something when Dennis started asking me questions where the obvious answer was "yes." I have spent enough time in sales to know that this is a tried and true technique to curate an aligned mindset with your potential customer. By getting them to say "yes" early and often, you increase the chance of them saying "yes" to the big ask of buying whatever it is you're selling.

In this case, I answered "yes" to his questions and signed up for a 90-day mastermind program. Oddly enough, when I shared my reflections on this conversation with Dennis, he was quick to say he thinks of himself more as a "talent agent" and less of a "sales" person. By finding and cultivating talent and putting talented people in contact with one another, he has found a need to "sell" only on a rare occasion.

The initial program I bought into centered around optimizing the foundations of health, wealth, and relationships. Everyone came to the program with a 90-day goal. Each week we had to report on weekly milestones towards that goal, our progress, our failures, and then we received some additional programming and educational content from Dennis. After going through his program and then signing on to join STRIVENT as a Mastermind Facilitator, continuing to share what I have learned with others on their paths to personal mastery, I was finally able to interview Dennis for the podcast, and subsequently, this book.

His story is an interesting one and is one that I feel a lot of people can relate to. But where Dennis differs from most people is in his ability to execute on his ideas and to block out things from the surrounding world that do not align with his goals. He's absolutely a "ready, fire, aim" person — putting more weight on speed and on trying as many different ways as possible versus waiting for the perfect approach. This acceptance of failing fast and failing often has helped him fast-track his way to success. In the time it takes most people to take action on one idea, Dennis has already taken action on three. Or more.

It was about 13 years ago that Dennis got his first taste of entrepreneurship, when he began a residential painting business. Ironically, Dennis never painted a single stroke in the time he ran this company. Instead, he orchestrated a team of project managers, job foremen, and salespeople and built the company from nothing to a profitable enterprise. There was just one problem.

Dennis did not love paint.

Even though the business was viable from a financial perspective, it did not fulfill his inner creator. The way Dennis describes it, he's always felt a sense of greatness calling to him. A feeling that he's meant to do more. Especially more than simply orchestrating a team of house painters.

Unable to tamp down that feeling any longer, Dennis closed his business and embarked on a journey of self-discovery. After years of devouring every book he could get his hands on, Dennis arrived at his own personal mission statement:

"To inspire and empower others."

Dennis believes that if everyone across the world was able to actualize their full potential, our world would be a much better place. He also believes that the sharpest sword we can brandish against detractors like anxiety and depression is being in community. By doing his part to actualize his own potential and to help as many people as possible to do the same, he hopes to cause a ripple effect of positivity and goodness.

In pursuit of this mission, Dennis formed his first coaching company about eight years ago, with a focus on coaching men and assisting them in balancing their masculine and feminine energies. In the end, his idea of energy-balancing was a bit before its time and was not as successful, or sustainable, as Dennis had hoped.

After going back to the drawing board, and back to more books, he pivoted and formed a new coaching company — focusing on what Dennis calls adventure coaching. He led groups of clients all over the world on massive expeditions like climbing Mount Kilimanjaro in Tanzania. The idea was that in stepping outside of their physical comfort zones to scale and overcome physical obstacles and mountains, his clients would be empowered to do the same with their own, internal and self-limiting beliefs.

However, trekking across the globe with a pack of neophyte explorers proved itself unsuccessful. Without the ability to scale his services, the adventure coaching would not be profitable.

Once again, back to the drawing board.

STRIVENT is the result of Dennis' most recent iteration of a coaching endeavor. While traveling around the globe, he found that he constantly bumped into the same type of person. The loner creative/entrepreneur whose brain was never at rest and who was searching for new challenges and growth opportunities. These people often felt like outliers in their immediate communities. Dennis' goal was to create a new community without borders, where these people could come together and form a virtual village focused on holding each other accountable to their goals. Instead of fading into the backdrop of their immediate surroundings, these folks could push each other further and further through weekly video calls and ongoing goal setting and evaluation.

The name STRIVENT is a portmanteau for "Striving" and "Present," meaning that all aspects of the coaching community focus on helping members strive to be present in every moment and area of their lives. Contrary to popular belief, Dennis believes that focusing on showing up powerfully in the present moment is the best way to create the ideal future. An intense focus on the future only leads to missing out on the present. Likewise, dwelling on the past will keep you from appreciating the present. Dennis' view is that when we can truly tap into the present moment — an awareness of it and an appreciation for it — we can have everything we want out of life.

As mentioned earlier, in his own pursuits of personal mastery, Dennis has turned to a myriad of books spanning the self-help, business, psychology, and counseling genres. After consuming all of this content, building businesses, and even walking away from businesses, he soon found that the content he was looking for in a book did not exist.

So, he wrote it.

Dennis published *Impression: A Comprehensive Guide to Optimal Wellbeing* in May 2018. IMPRESSION is an acronym for the ten interrelated elements of wellbeing as identified by Dennis as a result from his variety of experiences:

Intellectual
Monetary
Physical
Restoration
Emotional
Social
Spiritual
Intimacy
Occupational
Nutrition

While Dennis was able to find content on each of these areas on their own, before publishing *IMPRESSION* he was not able to find a sole source which discussed the importance of a well-rounded approach to health. The book is available for purchase on Amazon, and I highly recommend it!

This is why I call Dennis "Mr. Action." While an infinite amount of people would recognize a knowledge gap and only muse on the idea of publishing a book. Dennis took action and made it happen.

TAKEAWAYS

Dennis' story is an excellent example of the marriage between Active and Passive Unseen Work. Before I interviewed him, I only saw the polished entrepreneur and business coach. Having difficult conversations, offering deep intellectual insights, and navigating business situations seemed to be second nature to him. In fact, when I asked him to describe his life so far in three words, his response was, *"Action, Action, Action."* However, when I dug deeper, I learned exactly how he developed this confidence, how he built it up one brick at a time.

Dennis contacts upwards of 30 different people a day to keep his sales funnel filled. Of those 30, around a dozen matriculate into phone conversations, and a handful become paying clients. That means that in one week he could speak with well over 200 people. And in one year — nearly 11,000.

All of those calls are an active measure to grow his business and fulfill his mission. However, each call also has a passive compounding effect on Dennis as a person. With each conversation, each acceptance, and each rejection he learns new ways to pick up on vocal cues from those he interacts with, what gets people excited, and also what falls flat. These micro lessons go to work for him in every other area of his life, passively compounding to bolster his Active Unseen Work in every other area.

Think about your own life — do you see rejection this way?

How often do we all let the negative thoughts and words of others ruin our day or derail us from our passions? As an entrepreneur, Dennis is used to hearing no, to encountering setbacks, to experiencing failures and navigating pivot-points; but, by keeping his mind strong and clear, he is able to overcome those bumps – simply stepping over them instead of letting them turn into things that set him back. He harnesses failure and turns each instance of it into a learning moment — fueling his forward momentum towards his larger mission.

I asked him how he addresses haters and his response was flawless. He said that he tells them he is simply, "not available to be talked to that way."

What clarity!

Just as Dennis harnesses rejection and failure in small one-on-one interactions, he also harnesses it on a macro level. It took him three businesses — his painting company, his men's coaching company, and his adventure coaching company — before finding the proper format with STRIVENT Coaching. And even then, he is constantly making small adjustments and course corrections to how he formats community interaction and the services he offers.

While Dennis was actively pursuing each business at those particular moments in his past, as he moved through life, each of these experiences passively compounded into the way he shows up as an entrepreneur and coach today. While he was in the trenches building each of them, he had no clue how those particular lessons would transfer to a future endeavor, but as he looks back it is absolutely evident. This is why we could all stand to reframe our approach to and view of failure. We'll get into that more in the coming pages.

CHAPTER 19:
MASTERING YOUR UNSEEN WORK

As we laid out in the beginning of this section, the three different types of Unseen Work are not mutually exclusive. Active and Passive work do not exist in a vacuum. Generational Unseen Work is nothing more than the Active and Passive Unseen Work of those who have provided for our future opportunities, or the Active and Passive Unseen Work we put forth which becomes the foundation for future generations. Likewise, Passive Unseen Work is often a collection of Active Unseen Work; it is the cross-fertilization of unrelated events which culminate into moments of new opportunity. All of these ideas are meant to be complementary and not at odds with one another.

In fact, now that you've read these sections, I will bet you've started to notice the underlying forces of these three types of Unseen Work at play in your own life: how your Active Unseen Work towards individual goals, when looked back at over time, compounded into the accumulation of Passive Unseen Work towards an entirely different set of outcomes than you could have ever imagined. And how the foundation of your Generational Unseen Work has pointed you along certain paths without you even realizing it. Perhaps, by now, you've even developed additional types of Unseen Work based on your own experiences.

When contemplating how to approach the three types of

Unseen Work I've discovered throughout this book, I arranged each in a deliberate order. When presented in this way:

Generational
Active
Passive

We can take the first letter of each to form an acronym: G.A.P.

What I've come to realize through my purposeful interactions with people as a podcaster, and also through my daily interactions with strangers, co-workers, friends, and family, is that there is definitely a *gap* present in everyday life. Really, a massive rift. It separates those of us who read books such as this one and strive towards reaching personal mastery, from those who seem content to complain about the life that is happening to them versus the life they could be living or creating for themselves.

For some people, this is less of a rift and more of a puddle they can easily step over. Or, if it is in fact a rift. They don't look upon it with fear. Rather, they size up every inch of the crevasse and devise a method to successfully scale down into the depths of it all and triumphantly scale the opposing wall. This type of person is open to new ideas and easily picks up on the required thought patterns for success, realizing and then harnessing their Unseen Work. For others, a platform four times the expanse of the Golden Gate Bridge would be required to bring them over to this way of thinking. Even if you served that option up on a silver platter, they would see every reason why they could fail, instead of how they could be victorious.

Be brutally honest with yourself: which type of person have you been up until this point?

If, upon sincere reflection, you can admit that you routinely fall into the negative-thinking camp, do not worry. You can choose to draw a line in the sand and make today, and every day after, into an opportunity to choose your extraordinary self. If you feel like you're already there, don't get too comfortable, break into a victory dance, or pat yourself on the back too hard just yet. You might just fall into that gap rather than crossing it. Even when we're diligent about staying on the right path, it's easy to glance up and find that we've begun to stray. Now that we're all students of Unseen Work and possess an awareness of the rift standing between the current version of ourselves and our extraordinary selves, it's time for the real work to begin.

A simple awareness of the types of Unseen Work at play in our lives is not enough. We still need to build our bridges to cross that gap. And, like I said, for some of us it will require but one big step and you'll be there. For others, it will take years of work on our own self-limiting beliefs. But that's okay! Remember, it's what we do when no one is watching that defines how we are able to show up when the spotlight finally warms our skin.

The secret for bridging your own personal G.A.P. can be defined by a few additional acronyms.

F.L.I.P.

In many ways, your Unseen Work, and ability to bridge the G.A.P., is about failure. Failure is inevitable. As hard as we may try to escape it or push the thought from our minds it will always be there. When leveraged properly, it is the ultimate teacher. However, when avoided or rationalized, it is the ultimate excuse or crutch. As with everything in life, everything comes down to how we respond to what happens to us. In the course of our Unseen Work, when we find ourselves face-to-face with failure, we must F.L.I.P that failure. When we F.L.I.P. we:

Fail
Learn
Improvise
Pivot

Those who F.L.I.P. do not see failure as the end of the world.

Instead, they see it as an opportunity to learn something new, improve their skill set or mindset, and then take that learning and improvement and pivot their approach to try again. When we F.L.I.P. our failures, we turn weaknesses into strengths and forge ourselves into stronger beings who are prepared for life's next challenges. When we can do this, it's really not a failure at all. It's learning. We adapt and we pivot — moving on towards the next endeavor wiser for our previous attempts. Wearing our failures proudly on our sleeves. They become part of us and help define who we are and how we show up from then on.

I am no stranger to failure. I definitely don't always F.L.I.P. it to my advantage. However, I can think of a few defining moments in my life when I looked down the barrel of failure, tamped down my negative internal dialogue, and came out the other side a much better version of myself.

I was diagnosed with asthma at a very early age. Severe asthma. It was so bad that the doctors barred my mom from burning scented candles, and any dust-collecting trinkets had to be removed from my room. That meant no stuffed animals or drapes and allergen blocking covers on my mattress and pillows. If a protective bubble or ball could have been prescribed, chances are that 8-year-old me would have been navigating the world like a hamster.

It wasn't just scented candles or dust that aggravated my airways. It was exercise. While other kids could work up a healthy sweat running around and rough-housing, I would often be stopped short — having to take a break and suck down medicine through an inhaler. This, paired with my propensity to stuff my face with comfort food, meant that I wasn't the skinniest kid in school. It also meant that the Presidential fitness tests — a mix of rope climbing, pull ups, sit ups, pushups, and v-sit — became my own personal Hell. I can remember the jeering from my young peers as I finished the mile run in over fifteen minutes, truffle-shuffling across the finish line and nearly passing out from my lack of proper air flow:

Myles can't even run the mile.

Wow, he's so "biggs."

Biggs? More like HUGE.

I know — kids suck.

My parents, in all of their glory and adult wisdom, began taking proactive measures to help strengthen my lungs. I didn't realize it at the time, but they were pretty brilliant about it. In third grade, I began taking trumpet lessons. I also started competitive swimming in the summer. While I was not an all-star at either by any means, over time I became a decent musician — joining the marching band in addition to the concert band, and I even earned a spot in an auditioned jazz band, which was known amongst us band geeks as an elite group.

When it came to swimming, what began as a summer hobby as an 8-year-old, blossomed into a real passion of mine. I played team sports like baseball, soccer, and basketball as well, but swimming was the only one where how I performed was left solely up to me. I found it exhilarating to compete against my own best times and to see just how far I could push myself in practice and competition. While I ended up leaving traditional team sports behind, I earned a varsity letter all four years in high school for swimming and went on to compete as an NCAA athlete.

After years of swimming for at least two hours a day, sometimes eight times a week, that chubby kid who could barely run the mile, was swimming the mile with ease and earning spots atop the podium at championship swim meets. The baby fat melted away, as did the asthma and the jeering voices of my peers.

For me, this F.L.I.P. culminated when I finished running my first half marathon. I remember thinking that I wish those elementary school kids could see me now. I had finished the Pittsburgh Half Marathon in under two hours, with an average mile pace of under eight minutes per mile. A far cry from those

15-minute mile days. Instead of letting the teasing and "failure" get to me, I used it as fuel to prove people wrong. At least at first. Eventually, I found love in the disciplined routine of swimming. My driving force shifted from proving other people wrong to proving to myself how far I could go. I think when that transition happened is when the true F.L.I.P. occurred. That was the pivot point.

Another big F.L.I.P. for me centers around my shyness. My previous tendency towards introversion was for sure rooted in my insecurities around my physical appearance. While swimming helped to chisel my body, it also had the same effect on my mind. I realize now that competitive swimming is truly a sport that centers on mindfulness. In almost any other field of play, it is possible to talk openly with your teammates or hear direction from your coaches in the middle of the action. With swimming, your head is literally under water and all you can hear are muffled voices. You only get the occasional glimpse of people when you turn your head for a breath. You're left with just your thoughts for company.

I retreated there.

In high school, I kept to myself. Even though I was captain of the swim team, I didn't really have friends. I had plenty of acquaintances — team members, band mates, guys from my Boy Scout troop — but I kept everyone at an arm's length. I didn't even go to my own senior prom. This is all because, in my head, I was still replaying the bullies calling me fat and making fun of my name. I was inadvertently projecting a ton of my own issues onto my peers. I shied away from putting myself out there because I didn't want to go through the pain of getting made fun of all over again.

However, during my senior year of high school, as I began to gain more confidence in myself physically, emotionally, and mentally, I did begin to put myself out there more. I started a rock band with a few of my buddies from summer swimming and was the lead singer. I even dabbled with the bass guitar – albeit terribly. Our group played live shows, promoted ourselves heavily on Myspace, and even recorded a full album. It was a ton of fun.

I leveraged that confidence to audition for the small choir group that would stand in front of thousands of people at our high school graduation and sing the national anthem. I got it! Much to my amazement and everyone else's. There were for sure people who were pissed. I had never tried out for anything like that before and other people thought they would be shoe-ins for the spot I won.

Oh, well. Now, I was on a roll.

Bolstered even more by that personal victory, I used the recording of that performance at graduation and submitted it to the local minor league baseball team, the Lehigh Valley Iron Pigs. They were soon having a Boy Scout night and were looking for someone in Scouting to sing the National Anthem. Flash forward a few months and there I was, standing behind home plate, in my Eagle Scout uniform, with my face on the big screen and singing the National Anthem – by myself – in front of nearly 10,000 people. In a way, I am still sort of shocked that I actually made it through that experience. It was terrifying and rewarding all at once.

When I left for college, I made the decision to keep this kind of behavior going. I no longer wanted to fade into the background. I chose a small college, about half the size of my high school, and made the decision that everyone would know who I was. I became captain of the swim team, President of my fraternity, held positions in student government, got an on-campus job, was assistant manager of the radio station, and more. I used my positions in each of those areas to challenge the status quo.

And today, here I am, I've managed to keep the trend alive. I talk weekly to thousands of people with my podcast, I run a successful coaching business, I have a successful TEDx talk on YouTube, and I have written the book you are now reading.

Ok, I have to admit, as I wrote these words, I couldn't help but feel a sense of pride. It's easy to forget just how much I have been able to accomplish and how far I have come.

After falling in love with seeing how far I could push myself in the pool, I've transferred that same mindset to every area of my life and enjoy recording new personal bests. I'm not using myself as an example to be boastful or arrogant. I'm using myself to make a point. Anyone can do this. Anyone can F.L.I.P. (at any time). *Anyone.* For good measure, let me say that again – anyone. I'm repeating myself here because I know that as some of you are reading this, you're already discounting the reality that you could achieve all of your own big dreams. But, I promise, once we purge ourselves of the negative, self-limiting bullshit in our brains, we can realize that the world has been there all along, just waiting for us to show up and grab it.

I alluded to this in the introduction, but perhaps the best example of the intense patience this art of F.L.I.P.-ing requires doesn't come from any one person, especially not from me, but instead comes to us from mother nature.

As mentioned earlier in this book, I'd like you to consider bamboo. It's an incredibly versatile plant that is used for everything from building structures to making clothes. But, if you were to plant a bamboo seed yourself, it could take up to five years of watering and soil cultivation before you saw any sprouting begin. During this time your neighbors, friends and family may laugh and question why you're wasting your time on something that's obviously not working.

But, when five years and one day comes along, that plant, which has been growing an extensive root system beneath the surface for five, seemingly uneventful years, can grow to be up to 80 feet tall in just six weeks. That's nearly two feet every single day! It's the Unseen Work that happens beneath the soil that propels this exponential growth. After seeing this intense amount of growth over such a "short" period of time, those same neighbors, friends, and family will not be laughing anymore. In fact, growing bamboo will become the newest craze. People will be beating down your door to learn your secret for such an "overnight success."

When it comes to this idea of success, we've all been

introduced to the idea that we can do anything we put our minds to. Well, I have news for you: this idea – at face value – is a complete lie. It's a rationalization that makes it acceptable to believe we can sit on the couch and think our dreams into existence. If we are to truly "put" our minds "to" something — that means taking action. Simply having an idea or just planting a seed isn't enough. If I had only thought about joining the swim team, running a half marathon, singing the national anthem in front of thousands, applying for a TEDx talk or writing this book, chances are you would have never heard my name. I mean – really – how many things have you accomplished by simply *thinking* about them?

Strong action taken on your ideas, while you are Unseen, will directly affect how you show up when your moment to be seen arrives. It's all about growing that root system beneath the surface to support what others see above the soil.

If we were to only focus on the idea of having an 80 feet bamboo tree, but then took no action and did not focus on enjoying the disciplined routine required to make it a reality, not only would we fail in growing the tree, but we could spend five years wrestling with self-doubt, anxiety, or even depression. We might even quit this thing that's obviously not working. Or making any money – yet! 'Yet' being the key word. Because one day, the payoff will be there (money or otherwise), as long as we show up powerfully every day.

Throughout all of this Unseen Work, it's easy to focus solely on external voices, pressures, and sources of negativity. It's comfortable. But, in reality, our internal dialogue can be the most damning. We can beat ourselves up better than anyone.

It may have been a group of grade school bullies making fun of me after that fifteen-minute mile, but I am the one who put the jeering on repeat for years inside of my own head.

These thoughts, these voices inside our heads, are perhaps the most common type of Unseen Work. The things we tell ourselves and no one else. These unseen thoughts become our unseen beliefs, our unseen beliefs affect our unseen actions and our unseen actions determine our level of success. Ultimately, they determine whether we ever cross the threshold from unseen to seen. Meaning, if we do not F.L.I.P. our mindsets, then our mindsets will flip us.

F.L.O.P.

The opposite of the F.L.I.P is the F.L.O.P. When we F.L.O.P., we deny our failures, point fingers at others, and pretend everything is ok. We rationalize things away until they only "feel" better. We don't learn anything. To me, this is the true definition of failure: when we rest on a mistake or misstep as a crutch and turn it into an excuse to not try again, instead of treating it as a setback on our much longer journey towards success. If we keep F.L.O.P.-ing, we are doomed to remain unseen forever. By F.L.O.P., I mean:

Fail
Lie
Obsess
Pretend

Those who F.L.O.P. are the Chicken Little's of the world — the sky is always falling. After they fail, they lie about it. They will continue to project an outward confidence, even though things didn't go the way they had planned, because they can't fathom admitting that they were wrong. While they show this false confidence on the outside, on the inside they are obsessing over the failure. They're beating themselves up, calling themselves stupid (and many other colorful names), and replaying the failure over and over in their mind; ultimately making it much worse than in reality. This is followed up by pretending the failure never happened. No learning takes place. Quite the opposite, everything is swept under the metaphorical rug of their perceptions and they trudge forward destined to repeat the same failure once again.

Sound familiar? I'm sure it does. Everyone is guilty of moments like this from time to time. If you're reading this and thinking to yourself that it doesn't apply to you, read it again. Then, read it a third time. Because if that's your mindset, it definitely applies to you. Until we can all acknowledge this, we'll continue to be stuck in our current situations and be doomed to repeat past failures. I'll use myself as an example once more. It seems only fair that I also share some negative baggage and not just my stories of perseverance or victory.

A little-known fact about me is that I know how to fly.

Before you jump to conclusions about my sanity, I'm not talking about anything comic book worthy here. No capes or superpowers involved.

I have a little over twenty hours in the left seat of a Cessna 172, single engine airplane. A few of those hours are even as a solo pilot. If your experience with flight has been confined solely to commercial, passenger aircraft, you have no idea what you're missing. I have never experienced anything more exhilarating than taxiing a plane on the runway while communicating with air traffic control, or that slight moment of fear after initiating the engine to full throttle and barreling down the runway for takeoff. In the moments after my first takeoff and landing, I swear I felt the full range of human emotions and wished I had packed an extra, dry shirt. Those first moments were second only to the sense of pride and total manliness I felt after performing a series of maneuvers without my instructor in the plane.

The downside is that roller coasters are now ruined forever.

I love flying, not only for the thrill and adrenaline burst, but also for the mental toughness it requires. When you're piloting a plane thousands of feet above the ground, with the roar of the engine muffled by your headset and the rapid-fire commands of air traffic control, it requires a meditative focus. If you bring the stress and worries of the day up in the sky with you, then you're likely to lose focus and make a mistake. Unlike driving a car, there's no pulling over and resting on a cloud until you regain your composure. The art of flying requires you to be one hundred percent in the present moment. A rare thing for us in our age of constant technological distractions.

Seriously, if you haven't tried this before, you should. Even if it is just once. Call your local regional airport and ask about what is commonly called a Discovery Flight – you will not regret it.

For all that love of flying I've just expounded upon, I still carry just a student pilot's license in my wallet. After getting to the halfway mark of flight school, I stopped. It's been over three years since my first solo flight. Even though those sensations still feel fresh and I love talking about it, each time I do, I feel the sting of defeat. I feel like an imposter. I can rationalize it away – and believe me I have – and say things like:

Come on Myles, your son was born halfway through your training, and it's not smart to fly while sleep deprived from a newborn.

Is flying really practical? Lessons are expensive and you have diapers to buy!

Well, it made your wife nervous so it's best to just stop and not freak her out.

What would you even use a pilot's license for anyway?

That's just a sampling, folks. That's that inner voice that we all know so well. In reality, I could have scheduled lessons around my son's sleep schedule or on days when I felt rested. I could have prioritized other spending habits to afford the lessons. Even if it made everyone in my life nervous (not just my wife) flying is one of the most regulated forms of travel and perfectly safe if you follow the detailed instructions at each step of your flight.

In reality, I failed at being a pilot. I F.L.O.P-ped.

I failed at continuing to register flight time. I lied to myself about the reasons why, and I made up plenty of excuses. I obsessed over it mentally for months – playing an intense game of mind tennis over what to do next. Ultimately, I pretend I don't care about it because that's easier than admitting that I really wish I had finished. If I ever do finish, I can rewrite this section and count my years of time outside of the cockpit as a setback on my path to ultimate success, but for now "Myles the pilot" sits firmly in the F.L.O.P. column on my report card.

Another area where I seem to alternate between perfectly executed F.L.I.P. and grossly rationalized F.L.O.P. is in my health and fitness. In the previous section, I shared how I was able to F.L.I.P. my shyness and aversion to social situations through years of breath control with music and swimming, along with continuing to pursue activities that would force me into the social spotlight. After years of an intense focus on this, I graduated college and slipped into the routine of the "real world." At first, I was able to maintain my balance of work, play, and exercise. I joined a gym and took up running as an alternative exercise outlet after my years spent in the pool. All of this culminated in running two half marathons and successfully maintaining my swimmer's physique for two full years removed from college and the sport.

Throughout this time, I applied the same mentality that had made me successful in college and in athletics to my career. I volunteered for extra assignments, worked through lunches, stayed for hours longer than required, worked on weekends, and accepted tasks out of state which required occasional bouts of travel. It didn't happen all at once, but I slowly found that the time I had available for long runs grew shorter and shorter. I would come home absolutely exhausted and instead of running six miles, I would drink six beers. This had the double effect of relaxing my body and also my mind – which had begun to race uncontrollably through everything I had on my plate.

Eventually, all of that hard work paid off, and I was promoted. Not just once, but twice in the course of two years. In my mid-twenties I found myself on top of the corporate ladder. It was everything I had been working so hard for. It definitely didn't feel like a failure.

However, these professional victories had come at a steep personal cost. I hadn't stepped foot in a gym or laced up running shoes in over three years and the scale was showing me numbers that started with a two for the first time in my entire life. But that still wasn't enough for me to change my behavior. The real eye opener wouldn't come until my wife was pregnant with our first child.

As someone who loves to fix things and situations, not being able to help my wife in some areas of her pregnancy was hard for me. I wanted so much to take her pain and discomfort on as my own, but I couldn't. However, one thing I could do was join her in solidarity and abstain from alcohol. In those nine months, I lost over forty pounds. Forty pounds! Just by drinking water and not beer, wine, or bourbon. That showed me just how much the stress of work was getting to me. I used to turn to alcohol because I liked the taste, I enjoyed learning about the process of how it was made and visiting local establishments for social outings. But my newfound sobriety helped me to realize that I was using it as an emotional crutch. That was not OK. I had F.L.O.P-ped without even realizing it.

I had failed to maintain balance in managing my work life and personal life. I lied to myself and said that I was just doing what I had to do and that as soon as I was established in my new executive role at work, I would work out again. I obsessed and beat myself up about my weight in my head and pretended it wasn't a big deal. But it was. I realized that if I did not make a change, I would end up overweight, stressed out, and unhappy. That was not the kind of employee I wanted to be or the husband I wanted to be. It damn sure wasn't who I wanted to show up as in my new role as a father.

Right now, some of you may be arguing that this isn't a F.L.O.P. at all. By me realizing I didn't like this aspect of my situation, it's not quite a failure but the start of a potential F.L.I.P. I can see where you're headed and you're not entirely wrong. But you're also not entirely right.

By this logic there wouldn't be any F.L.O.Ps. In my experience, it's rare that someone realizes a failure and then decides to happily make the same mistake over and over. Once the realization hits, behavior is altered. Even if a full F.L.I.P. does not occur, powerful progress is made.

However, this is a F.L.O.P. because I consistently chose alcohol and stress over my own health and wellness. I chose it each day. For more almost three years. Yes, I realized it eventually. But only after I failed to properly prioritize my long-term health a few hundred times over. That's the F.L.O.P.

F.L.I.P. vs. F.L.O.P.

Like the beach footwear, F.L.I.Ps and F.L.O.Ps often occur close together and work in tandem; you can't move forward without both, and you don't hear the sound of one without passing through the other first.

In the end, it's your attitude toward both occurrences that matters most. It's easy for us to get cocky and comfortable in our ability to channel failure as a method for achieving success. This cockiness often leads to the realization that we're kissing the pavement after an intense F.L.O.P. Fortunately, the opposite is true. When we roll over and stop kissing asphalt, something often ignites internally, and we vow to never wind up on our backs ever again.

By now, I hope you have noticed how each of these options begins with failure. Whether we F.L.I.P. or F.L.O.P., we all experience what we deem to be failures. There is no escaping it. It's what makes us human. While we cannot always control the cards we are dealt, we absolutely control how we respond to the external forces of this world.

The difference between those who are able to bridge the G.A.P. and those who are doomed to build ramshackle bridges, which cave in and send them into freefall, is what they choose to do after failure. How we react to these setbacks, which often take place in that bubble of invisibility — in our Unseen Work — will decide how we react to setbacks when we step into the spotlight. Everyday we can choose whether or not life is simply happening to us and is out of our control. The true magic happens when we realize that we are happening to life.

Remember:

When we F.L.I.P. our failures, we turn weaknesses into strengths and forge ourselves into stronger beings who are prepared for the next challenges life decides to throw at us. When we can do this, it's really not a failure at all. It's learning.

But:

When we F.L.O.P., we deny the failure, point fingers at others, and pretend everything is ok. We don't learn anything. We rationalize it away until it "feels" better. If we keep F.L.O.P.-ping, we're doomed to remain unseen forever.

If you go back and re-read the examples and stories of people from the preceding pages, you will see instance after instance of them utilizing a F.L.I.P. mentality. You can be sure they have also had a F.L.O.P. from time to time. But what matters is the option we choose to identify with and continue to come back to. It's dangerous to let either type of experience define who we are as a person. These things are not who we are. They are things. They are events. They are not our identity.

It's possible to fail at something without being a failure. It's possible to be successful at something without being a success. The quality of our lives is determined by how each of these moments compound and build off of one another, what we choose to take from them, and if we continue to take steps forward.

As we move forward, we're often told to leave the past in the past. However, how we show up today and who we'll be tomorrow are a direct result of our past actions. A better saying would be to not let the past hold you back. Instead of wearing it around your neck like an anchor or perverse badge of dishonor, bring it along with you for the next chapter. Treat it as a friendly companion. Keep it in your back pocket like the Swiss Army Knife of experience that it is and use it when situations demand it. Leverage it. Build on it.

In the story I shared about my inability to balance my professional and personal endeavors, I had absolutely found myself kissing concrete. However, even though I had F.L.O.P.-ped, and had been doing so for years without realizing it, I made the decision to F.L.I.P. that F.L.O.P. and, like the footwear allows, chose forward momentum.

I quit drinking.

I quit my job.

I walked away from a career I had built up with a company for nearly ten years and transitioned into another industry all together – one that better fit my personality and my love for creative endeavors. Day one of my new job was also day one of a new gym membership. I'm now in better shape than I ever was as a swimmer and will go into my thirties with defined abs for the first time in my life. Boom!

Like I've already said: if I can do it, anyone can do it. It's not always comfortable, but if you're serious about taking control of your life and owning every part of it – the bad along with the good – you'll find a way to stop making excuses and to start taking action.

Dave, Ashley, and Dennis were all able to bridge the G.A.P. between Unseen Work and earning their moments in the spotlight. Each has battled criticism from external forces and have endured fierce internal battles. All three have each crossed over to the side of success.

If we dissect each of their stories, we'll find a common thread of vulnerability. Each of them acknowledges their weaknesses. But instead of letting these weaknesses, or their F.L.O.P.s consume them, they harness them into positive actions. It's this combination of embracing shortcomings, and then taking the actions required to F.L.I.P. them to your favor, that, when used properly, will allow anyone to vaporize whatever remains of their self-doubt. Once we can defeat that fiercest enemy – the part of ourselves that seems to enjoy mediocrity and laughs at our big ideas – anything is possible. *Anything.*

F.L.I.P. VS. F.L.O.P. WORK PROMPTS:

As you're considering your own journey and relationship with Unseen Work further, I recommend setting aside a solid day to work through these questions. Brew a pot of coffee, turn off your phone, listen to your favorite music, and do whatever else you need to in order to enter a flow state. If you do this right, you'll be extremely uncomfortable. It may be one of the few times you've been completely honest with yourself in a long time – if not ever.

Devote an entire page of your journal to answering each of the following questions:

1. When you're presented with adversity or a big failure what's your initial reaction?
2. When you F.L.O.P., do you search for the teachable moment and a chance to dig deeper, work harder, alter a limiting behavior and charge forward once more?
    a. Or do you get defensive, lie about what you're actually working on or towards, point fingers at others, and tell yourself additional strings of fallacies to ease your own guilt or shame?
3. How do you want to approach future failures? What do you want your new relationship with failure to look like?
4. When was the last time you F.L.I.P.-ped?
    a. Is there a formula in that experience that you can crystallize and then replicate?
5. How can you help others around you F.L.I.P. instead of F.L.O.P.?
    a. How might this focus on helping others, help you?

Get ready, it's about to get even more uncomfortable. You've looked into the mirror and seen your true self, and now it's time to share it with someone else. This entire book, all of the journaling exercises and mindset challenges have been leading to this assignment in vulnerability.

NOTE: You don't have to sort through these prompts alone! Head over to www.mylesbiggs.com for information on the Unseen Work Mastermind. You can request more information, join the waiting list, and get access to a community of like-minded people who are putting in their Unseen Work – just like you.

MY CHALLENGE TO YOU:

Pick someone in your life you trust completely. Share with them that you're working to uncover the Unseen Work in your life. Share with them how you believe that you can use past or current failures to fuel future success.

Read them what you've written.

Then, ask them to answer the same prompts, not about themselves, but about you.

This will be powerful. It's not easy to hear the hard truth, especially from someone you trust, love and respect. But chances are, what you'll hear isn't going to be all bad. Remember, our own internal dialogue is often more damning than anything an outsider can place on us. Chances are, you will hear from this confidant that, in their eyes, you have already achieved much of what you want to accomplish when you answered the question about how you'd like to show up for yourself and your relationship with failure. You just needed someone to hold up the mirror and show you the beauty they see. Not the falsehood you've been hiding behind.

CONCLUSION:

So, now that you've had an introduction to the ideas of Generational, Active, and Passive Unseen Work and understand the power of both the F.L.I.P. and F.L.O.P. models – what next? Well, that's really up to you.

As odd as this may sound, as this book begins to draw to a close, it's my sincere hope that you now have more questions than you did when we embarked on this journey together. If you picked up this book in search of THE answer, the magic words that would leave you enlightened and able to pursue your own brand of world domination — I'm afraid you will finish this book without finding it. In reality, receiving THE answer never brought anyone true fulfillment. Life is not about absolute answers. Life is about learning how to ask the right questions. The right questions of others, sure, but most importantly the right questions of ourselves. When you can be honest with yourself and challenge your own mind to ask and answer the right types of questions, you'll find that you've always had what you needed to obtain your greatness and to become your best self.

As we've discussed, your thoughts and your mindset remain the truest form of Unseen Work. Each minute of every day presents you with the choice of how you will use them to your fullest potential. How you choose to show up for yourself, the questions you ask of yourself, the standard you hold your own mind to, will be what either holds you back or launches you forward toward your goals. In this way, Unseen Work is simply another phrase for our pursuit of self-mastery. Other people call similar ideas by different names and that's OK. Again – there is no one answer or one right answer.

As we complete this journey together, I urge you to remember the metaphor of the bamboo seed. It takes five years of intense focus and patience, but the payoff is exponential. Your Unseen Work is the same way. Do not simply return this book to a shelf and consider your task complete. It will be tempting to F.L.O.P. back on the couch and simply ponder the worlds of could-be and should-be. Remember that putting your mind to something, just like performing a F.L.I.P., means taking deliberate and calculated action.

Use your new awareness of these ideas to build on both the advantages and disadvantages bestowed upon you from your ancestors. Use this as the foundation to actively pursue new endeavors and conquer your goals; all the while cross fertilizing your different interests in a form of passive compound interest which will lead to untold and unforeseen levels of success.

CONCLUDING PROMPTS:
1. Why do you think you can't do something?
    a. Is it because someone told you that you can't or because you've actually tried?
    b. And then, how hard did you really try? Did you F.L.I.P. or F.L.O.P?
2. What could happen if you gave yourself permission to be creative with your life and ignored the "rules?"
3. How can you create a new, Active pursuit by cross-fertilizing and leveraging more than one previous accomplishment?
4. What are some ways you could transfer what may feel like outdated experiences into the present day?
5. How have your ancestors influenced how you show up in your own life?

6. When you're on your deathbed and looking back on your life, what do you want to have been different about the world because of your existence?
    a. Now, how can you leverage Unseen Work to make that a reality?

Perhaps the most beautiful thing about your Unseen Work and invisible moments is that they belong wholly and solely to you. No one can pass judgement on them. They cannot be weighed, measured or compared against an arbitrary system. They remain pure. They are sacred. These moments should be guarded and treasured. There is power in the ability to stay on the sidelines until the right moment. Select yours wisely. Once you enter the spotlight, those selfish moments will become rare creatures.

When the moment does come, step forward with the knowledge of what you did to get there. You've earned it. Remember that, if your big goal is to be seen, you need to F.L.I.P. your F.L.O.P.s and adopt an underdog mentality in every journey you embark upon.

Be humble.
Be curious.
Be vulnerable.

And you will go far.

Do your Unseen Work, so that, when you are seen, you have something to show for it.

ACKNOWLEDGEMENTS:
THE UNSEEN WORK OF WRITING THIS BOOK

This book was written in Airbnb's, in hotels, at the gym, on my lunch break, and on my iPhone. I wrote chapters in Minneapolis, Phoenix, Las Vegas, Pennsylvania, New Jersey and 30,000 feet in the air. I wrote in between speaking engagements at the International Builders Show, on the beach while on vacation, and in five-minute bursts when inspiration struck.

This particular section even began as a voice dictation on my phone while walking my dog before sunrise.

Ironically, I both began and finished this book in an airport. Continuing my irony, no matter how much I tell you about the moments spent writing or how certain ideas were hatched, or about all these people I've had the privilege of interviewing, that's all I can do — tell you. I can paint vivid images with my words in an attempt to bring these stories to life, but no matter how descriptive they are, you will never be able to see the real moments for yourself. To you, they remain forever unseen.

The bulk of these words were written in 2019 and it was originally edited and "ready to go" in late February 2020 with the intention to publish after my TEDx talk two months later. However, before any of that could happened, the world was thrust into a pandemic and COVID-19 forced all of us to come to terms with this idea of being unseen. The TEDx event was moved from April to October and this manuscript was shelved. As I reflect on all that's happened, I'm thankful for this forced pause. It allowed me to double-down on this idea of Unseen Work and focus on putting it into practice myself. Now more than ever, I believe everyone can, and will, benefit from the mindset shift that comes with leaning into the Unseen.

I'd like to use what remains of these pages in an attempt to shed light on the numerous heroes of this book whom you also cannot see. I used to believe that it would be possible to write a book completely alone – in a vacuum – away from outside influences and input. But that is, in no way, how I was able to write this book. It may be my name on the cover, but dozens contributed to its message.

I'll start by thanking my wife, Claire. While there will never be the proper words to fully convey either my love for her or my appreciation for the way she stands by all of my hair-brained endeavors, I will never stop trying to find those words. From late nights in the podcast studio and my constant stream of word-vomit as I become infatuated with a new idea, to weeks spent holding down the household while I traveled the country pursuing my passions, Claire has been my champion. She, for sure, prefers to remain Unseen, but I'll never un-see her. I love you Claire. Thank you.

Thank you to my parents, David and Kathleen, for raising me right and for being early editors of the book. I know that, with my somewhat blunt interpretations of history, I have often made them question their parenting skills, but I promise you two, you did good. I love you. I owe you more than I can say.

Thank you to the rest of my family, immediate and extended. I've interviewed many of them for the podcast, and their presence in my life has absolutely influenced this book, whether their stories made it into its pages or not. It always makes me smile when I see a family member sharing my content or commenting online, or asking me how the show, book, or TED Talk was progressing as I toiled away at wordsmithing. I'm a lucky man to have such a large group behind me. A special shoutout to my younger sister, Danielle, for helping me produce audio for the podcast and for being my go-to freelance designer. Thank you!

Thank you to every person who has ever been a guest on *Relish The Journey*. There are well over 100 of you out there in the world – infecting it with your awesomeness. It is a better place for having you in it, and I am a better person for having met you. Thank you for allowing me to be a steward of your stories.

Thank you to my editor, Kathleen Majorsky. It's a terrifying thing to hand over hundreds of pages to someone and then say, *have at it.* In my own mind, I loved what I had created, but I was completely unsure of how it would be received. I was especially unsure of how it would stand up to the red pen of a professional writer and editor. Kathleen was an absolute rock star to work with. Our shared Google Doc is full of sidebar debate and banter and an equal amount of her praise to balance out any criticisms. All-in-all, this is a MUCH better book now, than it was before Kathleen put me through my paces. I highly recommend her services to anyone else in need of a discerning eye, or to anyone who needs writing services in addition to editing. You can reach her directly by emailing **writerkmajor@gmail.com**.

And last, but not least, thank YOU. Yes, I'm talking to YOU, the one holding this book. Because what is an author, really, if no one reads their words? I appreciate you spending your hard-earned money and finite amount of time with these words. I would love to hear from you – to learn what you liked and to debate what you didn't – please feel free to email me at myles@rtjmedia.com.

Until next time everyone – Cheers!

UNSEEN WORK MASTERMIND:
THE BOOK MAY BE OVER,
BUT YOU'VE ONLY <u>JUST BEGUN</u>

I said at the beginning of this book that I didn't want you to treat this as a static object. I hope you highlighted passages EVERYWHERE, scribbled in the margins, and folded down corners to mark your favorite passages. With each section of journal prompts I also made a brief mention to the idea that you don't have to explore these ideas alone – there are people out there just like you, hoping to shift from Unseen to Seen and looking to turn their anonymity into a superpower.

The Unseen Work Mastermind is an 8-week program which brings the ideas in this book to life. Each week you'll hop on a Zoom call with me and a group of other people working on making the transition from Unseen to Seen.

Head over to www.mylesbiggs.com for information and to join the Mastermind waiting list. New cohorts are starting every month. Can't wait to see you there!

Made in the USA
Columbia, SC
13 November 2020

24426185R00105